DANISH:
AN ESSENTIAL GRAMMAR

Titles of related interest published by Routledge:

Colloquial Danish: A Complete Language Course
Danish Dictionary
Danish: A Comprehensive Grammar

Colloquial Norwegian: A Complete Language Course
Norwegian Dictionary
Norwegian: An Essential Grammar

Colloquial Swedish: The Complete Course for Beginners
Swedish Dictionary
Swedish: A Comprehensive Grammar
Swedish: An Essential Grammar

DANISH:
AN ESSENTIAL
GRAMMAR

Robin Allan
Philip Holmes
Tom Lundskær-Nielsen

London and New York

First published 2000
by Routledge
11 New Fetter Lane, London EC4P 4EE

Simultaneously published in the USA and Canada
by Routledge
29 West 35th Street, New York, NY 10001

Routledge is an imprint of the Taylor & Francis Group

© 2000 Robin Allan, Philip Holmes and Tom Lundskær-Nielsen

Typeset in Times by
Florence Production Ltd, Stoodleigh, Devon

Printed and bound in Great Britain by
Biddles Ltd, Guildford and King's Lynn

British Library Cataloguing in Publication Data
A catalogue record for this book is available from the British Library

Library of Congress Cataloging in Publication Data
A catalogue record for this book has been requested

ISBN 0–415–20678–2 (hbk)
ISBN 0–415–20679–0 (pbk)

CONTENTS

Preface   xii
Symbols and abbreviations used in the text   xiii

1   PRONUNCIATION   1

Vowel sounds

   1   Vowels and their pronunciation   1
   2   Vowel length and spelling   3
   3   Diphthongs   5

Consonant sounds

   4   Stops: **p, t, k**   5
   5   Stops: **b, d, g**   6
   6   **s, c, sc, x, z**   7
   7   **f, h, j, sj, sh, ch**   8
   8   **l, n, ng, nk, r, v, w**   8
   9   Syllable loss and vowel merger   9
  10   Pronunciation of some frequent words   9

The glottal stop

  11   The glottal stop ('stød')   10
  12   Inflected forms – 'stød' variations   11

Stress

  13   Stress   13
  14   Stressed in the clause   13
  15   Unstressed in the clause   14
  16   Two-word stress   15
  17   Stressed and unstressed syllables   16
  18   Stressed prefixes   17
  19   Stressed suffixes   17
  20   Unstressed prefixes   17
  21   Unstressed suffixes   18

2 NOUNS   19

Gender

22   Gender   19
23   Gender rules   19

Plurals

24   Plurals and declensions   22
25   Predicting plurals   22
26   Plurals in **-(e)r** (**en gade – gader**; **et billede – billeder**)   23
27   Plurals in **-e** (**en dag – dage**; **et hus – huse**)   24
28   Zero-plural (**en sko – sko**; **et år – år**)   25
29   Plurals with a vowel change (**en tand – tænder**)   25
30   Plurals of nouns in **-el**, **-en**, **-er** (**en søster – søstre**)   26
31   Nouns doubling the final consonant   26
32   Plurals of loanwords   27
33   Count and non-count nouns   27
34   Nouns with no plural form   28
35   Nouns with no singular form   28
36   Differences in number   28

The genitive

37   Genitives   29

Articles

38   Articles – form   30
39   Article use – introduction   31
40   Article use – end article in Danish, no article in
     English   32
41   Article use – no article in Danish, definite article
     in English   33
42   Article use – no article in Danish, indefinite article
     in English   33
43   Article use – end article in Danish, possessive pronoun
     in English   34

3 ADJECTIVES   35

44   Adjectives in outline   35

Indefinite declension

45   Indefinite form – regular   35
46   Indefinite form – neuter same as common gender   36

47   Variations in plural/definite   37
48   Indefinite form – special cases   37
49   Adjectives doubling the final consonant in the plural   38
50   Indeclinable adjectives   38
51   Indefinite constructions   39
52   Agreement and lack of agreement   40

Definite declension

53   Definite constructions   41
54   Adjectival nouns   42
55   'The English' and other nationality words   43

Comparison

56   Comparison – introduction   44
57   Comparison with **-ere**, **-est**   45
58   Comparison with vowel change and **-(e)re**, **-(e)st**   46
59   Irregular comparison   46
60   Comparison with **mere**, **mest**   47
61   Similarity, dissimilarity and reinforcement   48
62   Inflexion of the superlative   48
63   The absolute comparative and absolute superlative   49

4   **NUMERALS**   50

64   Cardinal and ordinal numbers   50
65   Major uses of cardinal and ordinal numbers   52
66   Time by the clock   53

5   **PRONOUNS**   55

67   Personal and reflexive pronouns – form   55
68   Use of personal pronouns   55
69   Uses of **det**   56
70   Reflexive pronouns   58
71   Reciprocal pronouns   59
72   Possessive pronouns   59
73   Non-reflexive and reflexive possessives: **hans** or **sin**?   60
74   Demonstrative pronouns   63
75   Relative pronouns   64
76   **Der** or **som**?   67
77   Interrogative pronouns (**hv-** words)   68
78   Indefinite pronouns   69

6   VERBS   75

Verb forms

79   Verb forms in outline   75
80   First conjugation   76
81   Second conjugation   76
82   Third conjugation   78
83   Fourth conjugation – introduction   78
84   Fourth conjugation: stem vowel in **-a-**   79
85   Fourth conjugation: stem vowel in **-e-**   79
86   Fourth conjugation: stem vowel in **-i-**   79
87   Fourth conjugation: stem vowel in **-y-**   81
88   Fourth conjugation: stem vowel in **-æ-**   82
89   Fourth conjugation: stem vowel in **-å-**   83
90   Fourth conjugation: verbs with the same stem vowel
       in all forms   83
91   Infinitive   84
92   Past participle   86
93   Present participle   88

Tenses

94   Present tense   90
95   Past tense   90
96   Perfect tense   91
97   Past perfect tense   92
98   Future tense   93
99   Differences in the use of tenses   93

Mood

100   Mood and modal verbs   94
101   Imperative   97
102   Subjunctive   97

Types of verb

103   Transitive, intransitive, copula and reflexive verbs   98

-s Verbs and the passive

104   -s forms, deponent and reciprocal verbs   100
105   The passive   101

Compound verbs

106   Compound verbs   104

7 ADVERBS   106

  107   Adverbs – form   106
  108   Comparison of adverbs   107
  109   Use of adverbs   108
  110   Adverbs indicating location and motion   108
  111   Some difficult adverbs   110

8 PREPOSITIONS   112

  112   Prepositions – introduction   112
  113   The most common Danish prepositions   115
  114   **af**   117
  115   **efter**   118
  116   **for**   119
  117   **fra**   120
  118   **i**   120
  119   **med**   122
  120   **mod**   122
  121   **om**   123
  122   **over**   124
  123   **på**   124
  124   **til**   125
  125   **under**   126
  126   **ved**   127
  127   Common English prepositions and their Danish
        equivalents – summary   128
  128   Translating 'at', 'in', 'on', etc., as expressions of time   128
  129   Translating 'at', 'in', 'on', etc., as expressions of place   130
  130   Prepositions in expressions of time – summary   132
  131   Translating 'of'   133

9 INTERJECTIONS   135

  132   Interjections   135

10 CONJUNCTIONS   139

  133   Coordinating conjunctions   139
  134   Subordinating conjunctions   139
  135   Other subordinators   142
  136   Translating some difficult conjunctions   143

11   WORD ORDER AND CLAUSE STRUCTURE   146

137   Word classes and clause elements   146
138   Clause types   146
139   Main clause structure   148
140   Link position   149
141   Extra positions   149
142   Real subject and formal subject   150
143   Finite verb   150
144   Non-finite verb   151
145   Clausal adverbial   151
146   Other adverbials   152
147   Objects and complements   152
148   Passive agent   154
149   Topicalisation   154
150   Light elements   156
151   Position of **ikke** and negative elements   156
152   Passive transformation   157
153   Existential sentences   158
154   Subordinate clause as an element in the main
        clause   159
155   Main clause structure – an extended positional
        schema with examples   160
156   Subordinate clause structure   161
157   Independent clauses   163
158   Cleft sentences   163
159   Three types of subordinate clause with main clause
        structure   164
160   Major word order and clause structure problems
        – summary   165

12   WORD FORMATION   167

161   Introduction   167
162   Compounding   167
163   Affixation   169
164   Abbreviation   173
165   List of common abbreviations   173

13   ORTHOGRAPHY   178

166   The alphabet   178
167   **Aa, Å, aa, å**   178

168   Small or capital letters?   178
169   Word division   179

14   PUNCTUATION   181

170   Punctuation marks   181
171   The comma   181
172   The full stop   183
173   The exclamation mark   183
174   Direct speech   183
175   The apostrophe   184
176   The hyphen   184

Linguistic terms   185
Danish, Latin and English linguistic terms   191
Short bibliography   194
Index   196

PREFACE

We have two aims with this book. First, we want to provide learners of Danish with a concise description of the structure of Danish phonology, morphology and syntax, as well as a brief account of orthography, punctuation and word formation. Second, we try to describe in greater detail those areas of Danish structure that in our experience tend to pose special problems for learners whose first language is English. To help learners, most of the examples have been translated.

The 'new comma', as recommended by the Danish National Language Council, has been used throughout.

The book is largely traditional in its approach and terminology, but a number of the terms used are explained in a separate glossary of 'Linguistic Terms' at the end.

The various tables and diagrams are intended to make the book easy to use; in many cases it will be possible for the learner to predict word forms and clause patterns from just a few rules. The 'Index' contains paragraph references both to linguistic concepts and to some Danish and English keywords and their uses, and together with the 'Contents' this should normally serve as a starting point for any search.

Learners progressing to an intermediate level or simply wanting more thorough explanations of specific points may wish to consult our much more detailed *Danish: A Comprehensive Grammar*, Routledge, 1995, reprinted with changes in 1998.

We would like to thank Henrik Galberg Jacobsen for his invaluable comments, especially on the chapter on pronunciation, and we are extremely grateful to Dinah Bechshøft at the Danish Ministry of Education for financial support in the preparation phase. Other colleagues and students have provided helpful suggestions, but any errors are ours alone.

The authors primarily responsible for the individual chapters of the book are as follows: Chapters 1, 2, 3, 4 (PH), Chapters 5, 6 (TLN), Chapter 7 (RA), Chapters 8, 9 (TLN), Chapters 10, 11 (RA), Chapters 12, 13, 14 (PH).

Robin Allan, Philip Holmes and
Tom Lundskær-Nielsen
November 1999

SYMBOLS AND ABBREVIATIONS USED IN THE TEXT

[ ]	phonetic script
[i:]	long vowel
'kalde, **stu'dere**	stressed syllable
2 + syllables	two or more syllables
kolleg(a)er, **(at)**	letter, syllable or word may be omitted
ring*er*	stem **ring** plus ending *-er*
der/som	alternatives
x → y	**x** becomes **y**, e.g. when an ending is added
MC, SC	main clause, subordinate clause
hv- question	question introduced by an interrogative pronoun or adverb (**hv-** word)
pron.	pronunciation
cons	consonant
⊗	'plus zero', i.e. no ending is added to a word form
*	incorrect form or ungrammatical construction
S	subject
FS	formal subject
RS	real subject
InfS	subject of an infinitive
SComp.	subject complement
O	object
DO	direct object
IO	indirect object
V	verb
FV	finite verb

intr.	intransitive verb
tr.	transitive verb
prep.	preposition
Prep.Comp.	prepositional complement
sub conj	subordinating conjunction
a	clausal adverbial (position)
A	other adverbial (position)
F	front position
k	link position (conjunctions)
X_1, X_2	extra positions
FE	first element (in a compound)
SE	second element (in a compound)

1 PRONUNCIATION

This brief account of Danish pronunciation uses a modified version of IPA (International Phonetic Alphabet).

VOWEL SOUNDS

1 VOWELS AND THEIR PRONUNCIATION

1 Unrounded vowels:

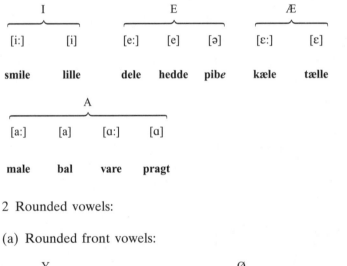

	I		E			Æ	
[iː]	[i]	[eː]	[e]	[ə]	[ɛː]	[ɛ]
smile	lille	dele	hedde	pib*e*	kæle	tælle

	A		
[aː]	[a]	[ɑː]	[ɑ]
male	bal	vare	pragt

2 Rounded vowels:

(a) Rounded front vowels:

	Y		Ø			
[yː]	[y]	[øː]	[ø]	[œː]	[œ]
hyle	fylde	føle	øl	gøre	børn

(b) Rounded back vowels:

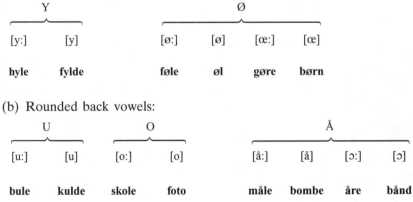

	U		O			Å		
[uː]	[u]	[oː]	[o]	[åː]	[å]	[ɔː]	[ɔ]
bule	kulde	skole	foto	måle	bombe	åre	bånd

Notes:

1 The pronunciation of the letters **i**, **o**, **u**, **y** when representing short vowels is often more open than is usually associated with these letters:

  finde ['fenə], **bombe** ['båmbə], **kul** [kål], **skylle** ['sgølə]

2 Pronunciation of **e**, **æ**, **a**, **ø**, **å** before and after **r** is more open than in other positions:

  long vowels: **ren**, **træ**, **fare**, **frø**, **gøre**, **får**; short vowels: **fred**, **fræk**, **fra**, **var**, **krølle**, **børste**, **rådhus**

3 The position of Danish vowels:

Unrounded vowels

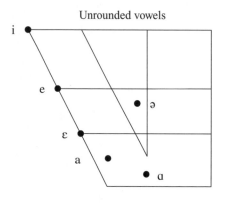

Rounded vowels

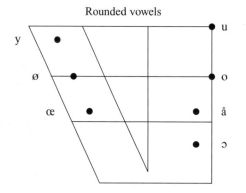

4 Vowels by articulation:

| | Front | | Back | |
	Unrounded	*Rounded*	*Unrounded*	*Rounded*
Closed	i	y		u
Half closed	e	ø		o
Half open	ε	œ		å
Open	a		ɑ	ɔ

5 Approximate equivalent to pronunciation (here 'English' = British English):

Long **i**	[iː]	ee in English 'bee'
Short **i**	[i]	i in English 'sin'
Long **e**	[eː]	No equivalent in English, cf. French 'les'
Short **e**	[e]	i in English 'if'
Unstressed **e**	[ə]	initial a in English 'again'
Long **æ**	[ɛː]	ai in English 'said'
Short **æ**	[ɛ]	e in English 'pet'
Long **a**	[aː]	a in English 'bad' but slightly more open
Short **a**	[a]	a in English 'hat'
Long (open) **a**	[ɑː]	a in English 'card'
Short (open) **a**	[ɑ]	ea in English 'heart', but shorter
Long **y**	[yː]	No equivalent in English, cf. German ü in 'Bühne'
Short **y**	[y]	No equivalent in English, cf. German ü in 'Glück'
Long **ø**	[øː]	No equivalent in English, cf. German ö in 'schön'
Short **ø**	[ø]	No equivalent in English, cf. French eux in 'deux'
Long (open) **ø**	[œː]	No equivalent in English, cf. French eu in 'leur'
Short (open) **ø**	[œ]	No equivalent in English, cf. French eu in 'neuf'
Long **u**	[uː]	oo in English 'room'
Short **u**	[u]	u in English 'full'
Long **o**	[oː]	No equivalent in English, cf. German o in 'froh'
Short **o**	[o]	eau in French 'beau'
Long **å**	[åː]	No equivalent in English, French or German
Short **å**	[å]	No equivalent in English, French or German
Long (open) **å**	[ɔː]	a in English 'all'
Short (open) **å**	[ɔ]	o in English 'hot'

Note: The pronunciation of **e** is very variable and difficult to predict. In unstressed syllables the letter **e** is pronounced as schwa [ə]:

gribe ['griːbə], **flue** ['fluːə], **gammel** ['gɑməl], **billede** ['beləðə], **værelse** ['vɛːrəlsə], **fælles** ['fɛləs]

-er often merges and is pronounced [ɔ]: **sommer** ['sɔmɔ], **søster** ['søsdɔ]
-re and **-rer** are pronounced [ɔ]: **lære** ['lɛːɔ], **lærer** ['lɛːɔ]

For the loss of **e** in the pronunciation of some words see **9**.

2 VOWEL LENGTH AND SPELLING

1 A double consonant or consonant group between two vowels usually indicates that the preceding vowel is short, a single consonant that it is long (but see **2.2** below):

Long	Short
VCV	*VCCV*
læse	læsse
lyse	tyske
kæle	vælte
smile	lille
lune	kunne
skrabe	krabbe

Exceptions:

1 Long vowel + double (long) consonant is found in some words in **æ-** (which is long): **æg – ægget, æt – ætten**, some words in **-dd, -tt: bredde, vidde, otte, sjette** and a few others: **hoste, påske**.

2 Vowels before **-gl, -gn** where the **g** is silent are long: **fugle, ligne**.

2 The single final consonants **b** and **n** usually follow a long vowel: **reb, gren**. But if the single final consonant is **m, p, t, k, g** (pronounced hard as [g]), **f,** the preceding vowel is usually short: **lam, krop, hat, blik, bryg, stof**. It is not always possible to detect whether the vowel is long or short from the written form, as one of the two consonants is usually dropped in final position in Danish. This is especially difficult in the case of **l, s**:

Long	Short
sal	smal
sol	øl
stil	til
hus	bus
las	glas

Only when these words are inflected (i.e. when a vowel is added after the consonant) can we determine from the single or double consonant what the vowel length is:

Long	Short
salen	smalle
solen	øllet
huse	busser
lasen	glasset

3 Final stressed vowels are usually long: **se, sy, tro, gå**.

Exceptions: These include some words usually unstressed in the sentence, e.g. personal pronouns: **du, vi, I, de**, the adverbs **nu, så**, and the interjection **ja**.

3   DIPHTHONGS

Danish diphthongs are of two kinds. Notice the spelling of these sounds.

- Diphthongs with [i] as their second component:

aj, **eg**, **ej**, **ig**	[ɑi]	**maj, leg, hej, mig, dig, sig**
øg, **øj**	[ɔi]	**løg, nøgle, høj, tøj, fløjte**

Rather rarely:

uj	[ui]	**huje**

- Diphthongs with [u] as their second component:

iv	[iu]	**ivrig, livlig, tvivl**
ev	[eu]	**blev, hev**
ev	[ɛu]	**evne, brev**
yv	[yu]	**syv, tyv**
øv	[øu]	**øvre, støv**
øv	[œu]	**støvle, vrøvl**
ov	[ɔu]	**lov, skov**
ag	[ɑu]	**hagl**
av	[ɑu]	**hav** (sea)
av	[au]	**gav**
og	[åu]	**bog, sprog**

CONSONANT SOUNDS

4   STOPS: p, t, k

1 There are nine stops in Danish:

	Unvoiced		Voiced
	Aspirated	*Unaspirated*	
Lip sounds (bilabial)	**p**	**b**	**m**
Tongue tip sounds (alveolar)	**t**	**d**	**n**
Tongue root sounds (velar)	**k**	**g**	**ŋ**

2 **p**, **t** and **k** in initial position before a full vowel are aspirated stops:

p	[p]	**passe, pose**
t	[t]	**tand, til**
k	[k]	**kirke, komme**

In all other positions (including after **s-** and when doubled) **p, t, k** are unaspirated stops and become [b], [d], [g]:

p	[b]	**spille, tæppe, stop**
t	[d]	**støj, rotte, kat**
k	[g]	**sko, lokke, tak**

This produces homophones, so that **lappe** and **labbe** are both pronounced as ['labə].

3 Notice the following special pronunciations and spellings in loanwords:

p- is silent in the group **ps-**	**psykolog, pseudonym**
qu [k]	**enquete, mannequin**
[kv]	**quickstep, quiz**
-t is silent in some French loans	**buffet, debut, filet**
-ti- [ʃ]	**funktion, information, station**

5   STOPS: b, d, g

1 The letter **b** is pronounced [b] in all positions: **bil, briller, dyb, skæbne, åben.**

2 The letter **d** is usually pronounced in one of three ways:

(a) 'hard' **d**   [d]   initially and before a full vowel:

dag, dusin, dø, djærv, drama, soldat, student, heldig

(b) 'soft' **d**   [ð]   after a vowel and when doubled:

mad, møde, tredive, smedje, bedre, sødme, hedde, sidde

Exceptions:

1 **d** is [d] in **addere, bredde, middag, vidde.**

2 **moder**, mother; **fader**, father; and **broder**, brother; are often abbreviated **mor, far, bror** in both pronunciation and spelling, but the **d** found in the plural forms of these words is pronounced [ð]: **mødre, fædre, brødre.**

(c) silent **d**:

(i) **d** is silent in the combinations:

-ld:	**ild, sild, kildre, melde**
-nd:	**mand, vind, dundre, kende**

d is, therefore, silent in words ending in **-ende: spændende, søskende, tyvende**:

-rd:	**bord, gård, gærde**

Exceptions:

1 **ld, nd, rd** are pronounced [ld] [nd] [rd] respectively when they are followed by **-ig, -isk**:

heldig, mandig, værdig (cf. silent **d** in **held, mand, værd**)
heraldisk, indisk, nordisk (cf. silent **d** in **alder, ind, nord**)

2 **ld** is pronounced [ld] in the following frequent words incorporating **-ldr-**:

aldrig, ældre, forældre, skildre

3 **nd** is pronounced [nd] in many words incorporating **-ndr-**:

andre, hindre, ændre

(ii) **d** is also silent in the combinations:

-**ds**: **spids, klods, vidste**
-**dt**: **fedt, godt, skidt**

3 The letter **g** is usually pronounced in one of the following four ways:

(a) 'hard' **g** [g]:

before a full vowel: **gæst, gade, liga**
when doubled: **kigge, lægge**
before -**t**: **vigtigt, vægt**
following a short vowel: **mug, myg, ryg**
(cf. inflected forms: **muggen, myggen, ryggen**)

(b) 'soft' **g** [j] (or silent) after **i, e, æ, a, y, ø**:

krig, steg (from the verb **stege**), **læge, dag, syg, søge**

(c) silent **g**:

(i) **g** is silent in the combinations -**lg** in some cases: **salg, valg**.
(ii) **g** is silent after **u**: **rug, uge, kugle**.
(iii) **g** becomes [u] after **ra, r, o, å: krage, sorg, bog, tåge**.

Note: Adjectives ending in -**g** do not have hard **g** in the neuter: **klogt** [klåud].

(d) Note also the following loanwords involving the letter **g**:

g [dj] in some English loans **gentleman, manager**
g [dʃ] in some English loans **image, management**
g [ʃ] in some French loans **aubergine, logi, regi**
g [ʃ] before **e** **bagage, budget, garage, genere, ingeniør, prestige**

-**gn** [nj] in some French loans **champagne, cognac**

6 s, c, sc, x, z

s [s] **se, sol, spille, glas, vise**

s	is usually silent in French loans	**apropos, en gros, pommes frites, succes**
-si-	[ʃ]	**division, pension**
c	[s] before **i, e, æ, y, ø**	**cirkus, præcis, pjece, cæsar, cykel, cølibat**
c	[k] in other cases and before **a, o, u**	**café, computer, curling, picnic**
sc	[s] before **i, e**	**science fiction, scene**
	[sg] in other cases	**scoop, score, mascara, screene**
x	[s] initially	**xenofobi, xylofon**
x	[gs] after a vowel	**sex, taxa**
z	[s]	**benzin, jazz, ozon, zoologi**
zz	[ds] in some Italian loans	**pizza, mezzosopran**

7   f, h, j, sj, sh, ch

f	[f]	**fem, fisk, kaffe**
f	is silent in	**af**
f	[u] in **af-**	**affald, afsked**
h	[h]	**hest, hotel, hus**
h	is silent in **hj-, hv-**	**hjem, hjul, hjælpe, hjørne** (15 words in all) **hvad, hvem, hvid, hvis, hvor, hvordan** (some 30 words in all)
j	[j] before a vowel:	**jakke, jord, kjole, stjæle**
j	[ʃ] in some French loans:	**jalousi, jargon, journalist**
j	[dj] in some English loans	**jazz, jeans, jeep, job, juice**
j	is silent in	**vejr**
sj	[ʃ]	**sjov, sjuske, sjælden**
sh	[ʃ] in English loans	**shampoo, shorts, sherry, finish**
ch	[ʃ]	**chauffør, chef, chok, match**

8   l, n, ng, nk, r, v, w

l	[l]	**lille, luft, plante, folk**
	often silent in	**skal, skulle, til, vil**
n	[n]	**nabo, sne, skinne, ven**
ng	[ŋ]	**seng, bange, finger, synge**
ng	[ŋg] stressed **g** or before **a, u, o**	**fungere, tangent, tango**
nk	[ŋk] stressed **k** or before a consonant or **a, u, o**	**blanket, Frankrig, banko**
nk	[ŋg]	**tank, enke, synke, tænke**

Note:

an	[aŋ]	in the following:	**balance, branche, chance, restaurant**
en	[aŋ]	in the following:	**engagere, konkurrence, pension**
on	[ɔŋ]	in the following:	**beton, jargon, kupon, perron, konkurrere**

r	[r]	**ravn, ride, rose**
r	[ɔ] in endings: vowel + **-r(e), -er**	**være, roser, sender**
r	is silent in French loans	**atelier, foyer**
v	[v]	**vask, vise, kvinde, svare, avis**
v	[u] (see **3**)	**hævn, tavle, sovs**
v	is silent in the ending **-lv**	**selv, sølv, halv, gulv, tolv**

Exceptions:

lv is pronounced [lv] in **hvælv, ulv** and in inflected forms: **selve, halve**.

w	[v] or [w]	**sweater, weekend, whisky**
w	[u]	**bowle, cowboy, show**

9   SYLLABLE LOSS AND VOWEL MERGER

1 Unstressed **e** [ə] in a medial syllable is often not pronounced:

interessant [intrə'san'd], **elleve** (or **elve**) ['ɛlvə], **mærkelig** ['maɔgli], **husene** ['hu:'snə], **lugtede** ['lågdð], **faldende** ['falnə], **cykelen** [or **cyklen**] ['syglən]

This also occurs in the present tense of certain common verbs, where a consonant + unstressed **e** is not pronounced:

beder ['be'ɔ], **klæder** ['klɛ:ɔ], **tager** [tɑ'], **bliver** ['bli'ɔ], **giver** ['gi'ɔ], **siger** ['si:'ɔ], **bruger** ['bru:ɔ], **spørger** ['sbœɔ], **bærer** ['bɛɔ], **skærer** ['sgɛɔ], **rører** ['rœɔ]

2 In rapid speech unstressed **e** [ə] tends to merge (i.e. adopt the same pronunciation) as adjacent vowels:

	Normal tempo	*Rapid tempo*
stue	['sdu:ə]	[sdu:u]
pige	['pi:ə]	[pi:i]

10   PRONUNCIATION OF SOME FREQUENT WORDS

Some words of high frequency are not pronounced phonetically. They include the following, which are often found in unstressed positions in the clause (see **13**).

Pronouns:

jeg	[jɑ]	**De**	[di]	**de**	[di]
mig	[mɑ]	**dig**	[dɑ]	**sig**	[sɑ]

Modal verbs:

kan	[ka]	**skal**	[sga]	**vil**	[ve]
kunne	[ku]	**skulle**	[sgu]		

Verbs:

have	[ha]	**blive**	[bli:]	**tage**	[ta]

Adverbs:

ikke	[eg]

Conjunctions, etc.:

og	[ɔ]	**at**	[ad] or [a]

Han lå *og* sov. / Hun sagde *at* hun ville komme i dag.

at as an infinitive marker [ɔ]:

Glem ikke *at* skrive.

Prepositions:

med	[mɛ]	**til**	[te]	**ved**	[ve]

THE GLOTTAL STOP

11   THE GLOTTAL STOP ('STØD')

1 In Danish the glottal stop or 'stød' (a sound like that found in Cockney 'bottle' [bɔ'l], 'water' [wɔ:'ə] or 'little' [li'l]) is a functional phoneme that is used to distinguish forms that are otherwise similar. To show this we list below some words with and without 'stød':

No 'stød'		'Stød'	
man	one	**mand'**	man
hun	she	**hund'**	dog
mig	me	**maj'**	May
møller	miller	**Møll'er**	(surname)
maler	painter	**ma'ler**	paints
byger (plural of **byge**)	showers	**by'er** (plural of **by**)	town
tanken (definite of **tanke**)	the thought	**tan'ken** (definite of **tank**)	the tank

Notice that in the last two cases 'stød' is used to indicate a monosyllabic stem (**by**, **tank**) and distinguish it from a bisyllabic stem (**byge**, **tanke**).

Note: The 'stød' is not found in some southern Danish dialects.

2 General rules for 'stød':
'Stød' can only be present:

- in stressed syllables (though not all stressed syllables)
- in voiced syllables.

Only two syllable types can therefore have 'stød':

- syllables with a long vowel; the long vowel then carries the 'stød':

  i's, bi'l, li'v, bageri', be'n, café', æ'g, hu's, ny', bå'd

- syllables with a short vowel + voiced consonant; the voiced consonant then carries the 'stød' (but 'stød' is not necessarily present in all cases):

  ler', mand', kam', skal', bord', grøn'

A word such as the adjective **let** can never therefore have 'stød', as it has a short vowel and voiceless consonant. Nor can, for example, **hat**, **hest**, **kop**, **snaps**.
   Notice that [b], [d], [g] are voiceless in Danish and do not take 'stød': **hoppe**, **otte**, **lægge**.
   It is primarily monosyllables that have 'stød': **barn'**, **frem'**, **gå'**, **grøn'**, **mund'**.

12   INFLECTED FORMS – 'STØD' VARIATIONS

The general rule is that inflexion does not alter the 'stød' pattern in inflected forms:

| with 'stød' | **hu's, hu'set; vej', vej'en; bo', bor'** |
| without 'stød' | **drage, drager; fare, farer** |

   In the summary below the focus is, however, on those cases where the pattern *does* change.

1 'Stød' in nouns:
Plural forms:
-r plurals: use is the same in the singular and the plural (either with or without 'stød' throughout).

-er plurals: 'stød' is lost in the plural of nouns ending in **-l, -m, -n, -r** + consonant: **en form', former**
'stød' is lost in the plural of nouns ending in **-nd, -rd** where the **d** is silent: **en stund', stunder**
'stød' is lost in the plural of nouns ending in **d** [ð]: **en tid', tider**

-e plurals: 'stød' is often lost in the plural: **et hu's, huse**

Zero plurals: use is the same in the singular and the plural (either with or without 'stød' throughout): **mu's, mu's.**

Nouns with end article:
Nouns ending in a voiced consonant may add 'stød': **gulv, gul'vet.**

2 'Stød' in adjectives:
Neuter form in **-t**: most adjectives do not change.
Adjectives ending in a stressed vowel lose 'stød' when adding the neuter ending: **fri', frit.**
Adjectives ending in **d** [ð] lose 'stød' when adding the neuter ending: **dø'd, dødt.**

Plural forms in **-e**:
Monosyllables generally lose 'stød' in the plural: **dum', dumme.**

Comparatives and superlatives:
Adjectives with 'stød' generally lose it in the comparative and superlative: **nem', nemmere, nemmest; se'n, senere, senest.**

3 'Stød' in verbs:
Weak verbs (Conjugations I, II, III) tend to lose 'stød' in the past tense if they already possess it in the infinitive or present tense.

Infinitive	Present	Past	Past participle	Meaning
bo'	**bor'**	**boede**	**bo'et**	live, stay
tale	**ta'ler**	**talte**	**ta'lt**	talk
dø'	**dør'**	**døde**	**død'**	die

Strong verbs (Conjugation IV): those with 'stød' in the infinitive or present tense tend to lose the 'stød' in the past participle.

stå'	**står'**	**stod'**	**stået**	stand
finde	**find'er**	**fand't**	**fundet**	find

-r stem verbs only have 'stød' in the past tense:

bære	**bærer**	**bar'**	**båret**	carry
fare	**farer**	**for'**	**faret**	hurry

Imperatives:

If the infinitive has a long vowel, 'stød' appears in the imperative: **købe, kø'b!**

If the infinitive has a short vowel with a voiced consonant, the consonant takes 'stød' in the imperative: **kalde, kald'!**

STRESS

13 STRESS

In Danish – as in English – there is an important distinction between words that have stress in the clause and those that do not. All the words that are significant for the meaning of a clause are stressed (see **14**). This is called clause stress. But different syllables within these stressed words may also be stressed. This is known as word stress. The method shown for marking stress is illustrated here:

Hun er 'nitten 'år og stu'derende.   She is 19 years old and a
student.

What follows is a series of lists for reference:

• of those types of words in the clause which have clause stress
• of those types of words which are usually unstressed
• of phrases with two-word stress
• of stressed and unstressed syllables within words
• of stressed and unstressed prefixes and suffixes within words.

14 STRESSED IN THE CLAUSE

Nouns

Nouns are usually stressed:

'Lis har 'købt et 'hus.   Lis has bought a house.
'Huset 'har et 'tag.   The house has a roof.

Exceptions:

Nouns expressing quantity:

et antal 'børn   a number of children

Titles before proper nouns:

direktør 'Nielsen   Director Nielsen

Verbs

Simple full verbs are usually stressed:

> **'Eva 'spiser og 'drikker 'hele 'dagen.**   Eva eats and drinks all
>   day.
> **'Eva 'drikker en 'øl.**   Eva is drinking a beer.

But verbs are unstressed when followed by a subject complement:

> **Hun blev 'syg.**   She fell ill.
>   SComp.
> **Han er poli'tibetjent.**   He is a policeman.
>   SComp.

Note: **er** is pronounced with a short [ɛɔ].

Expressions of manner, place, time (MPT-expressions)

These expressions usually have stress.

> **'Nu bor hun i 'Sakskøbing.**   Now she lives in Sakskøbing.
>   MPT   MPT
> **'Lukker for'retningen 'tidligt i 'dag?** Is the shop shutting early
>   MPT   MPT   today?

15   UNSTRESSED IN THE CLAUSE

Modal verbs and modal equivalents

> **'Svend vil være pro'fessor.**   Svend wants to be a professor.
> **'Hans gider ikke skrive 'brev.**   Hans can't be bothered to write
>   a letter.

*Pronouns and **hv-** words (interrogatives)*

jeg [ja], **du, han, hun, den, det** [de], **vi, I, De, de** [di] (I, you, he, she, it,
it, we, you, they)

> **Hvad 'sagde du?**   What did you say?

mig [ma], **dig** [da], **sig** [sa], **ham, hende, os, jer, Dem, dem** (me, you,
himself, etc., him, her, us, you, them)

Exception: When the object pronoun is in initial position or is contrasted, it acquires
stress:

'Ham elsker jeg (men 'hende synes jeg ikke om).   Him I love (but her I do not like).
(Jeg 'elsker ham.   I love him.)

Possessive pronouns when used with a noun:

min, din, sin, hans, hendes,   my, your, his, etc., his, her,
dens, dets, vores, jeres, Deres, deres   its, our, your, their

Det er 'vores 'hus.   It's our house.

Conjunctions

og [ɔ], men, at   and, but, that
da, når, om, hvis   when/since, when, whether, if

Han 'sagde at han drak 'gin   He said that he drank gin
og 'tonic.   and tonic.

16   TWO-WORD STRESS

Where two or more words belong together in one semantic unit, the last word in the phrase is stressed.

Preposition + noun

(Kig) i 'bogen.   **(De kommer) i 'dag.**
Look in the book.   They're coming today.

Indefinite article + noun

en 'bil   **et 'hus**
a car   a house

Verb + particle

gå 'ud   **vende 'om**
go out   turn round

Verb$_1$ + verb$_2$

Jeg skal 'gå.   **De var 'kommet.**
I must go.   They had arrived.

Infinitive marker + verb

at 'gå   **at 'komme**
to go   to come

Verb + complement

(Han) er 'høj.
He is tall.

(Hun) er 'slank.
She is slim.

end/som *+ the word compared*

(Han er højere) end 'Ole.
He is taller than Ole.

(Han er lige så ung) som 'hende.
He is just as young as she is.

Pronoun + adverb

dette 'her
this

de 'der
those

Time, measurement

klokken 'tre
three o'clock

(to) kopper 'kaffe
two cups of coffee

First name + surname

Anders 'Nielsen

17   STRESSED AND UNSTRESSED SYLLABLES

Many indigenous non-compounds with more than one syllable, and all those with unstressed **e** [ə], have stress on the first syllable and either secondary stress or no stress on the following syllables:

Stress on the first syllable:

**'cykel, 'venlig, 'huse, 'eng₁lænder, 'al₁tid, 'ejen₁dom
'skrive, 'skriver, 'skrivende**

Stress on another syllable:

- words with the prefixes **be-, er-, for-**: **be'retning** (account), **be'tale** (pay), **er'fare** (experience), **for'nemmelse** (feeling)
- words with the suffix **-ere**: **par'kere** (park), **stu'dere** (study)
- many foreign loans: **restau'rant** (restaurant), **re'vy** (revue), **universi'tet** (university)
- words with foreign suffixes: **regis'sør** (stage manager), **gym'nast** (gymnast), **musi'kant** (musician).

Compounds (words made up of two (or more) words) usually have stress on the first syllable: **'arbejds₁plads, 'morgen₁mad, 'skrive₁bord, 'læse₁bog**

Some problem words:

Many words that are familiar from English are, however, stressed differently from English:

> **chauf'før, choko'lade, demo'krat, demonstra'tion, direk'tør, fa'milie, fi'gur, institu'tion, interes'seret, journa'list, 'juli, ka'tolsk, kul'tur, littera'tur, milli'on, mi'nut, mo'del, na'tur, ner'vøs, passa'ger, poli'tik, por'tion, pri'vat, pro'gram, refe'rence, religi'on, stu'dent, toi'let, traditio'nel, vegeta'tion**

18   STRESSED PREFIXES

These include amplifying, negating and contrasting prefixes.

a-, ante-, anti-, eks-, hyper-, mis-, pseudo-, semi-, super-, ultra-, und-, van-, vice-, ærke-:

> **'asocial, 'antedatere, 'antisemitisk, 'eksmand, 'hyperaktiv, 'mistanke, 'pseudovidenskabelig, 'semifinale, 'supernova, 'ultrahurtig, 'undgå, 'vanvittig, 'vicedirektør, 'ærkedansk**

19   STRESSED SUFFIXES

Many of these were originally loan suffixes.

-abel, -al, -ance, -ant, -ast, -at, -ere, -esse, -graf, -grafi, -ik, -isme, -ist, -sion, -tet, -ør, -øs, -øse:

> **vari'abel, origi'nal, tole'rance, konso'nant, kon'trast, appa'rat, koncen'trere, stewar'desse, foto'graf, bibliogra'fi, repub'lik, tu'risme, receptio'nist, ekspan'sion, kontinui'tet, konduk'tør, gene'røs, mass'øse**

20   UNSTRESSED PREFIXES

These include many loan prefixes.

ab-, be-, de-, er-, for-, ge-, in-, (il-, im-, ir-), intro-, kom-, kon- (kol-, kor-), mono-, pan-, para-, peri-, poly-, trans-:

> **ab'norm, be'tale, degra'dere, er'hverv, for'stå, ge'mytlig, intro'duktion, inva'lid, kompag'ni, kon'cern, mono'pol, pante'isme, para'doks, peri'fer, poly'krom, trans'port**

Exceptions:
'in- to express negation: **'ineffektiv, 'intolerant**
'for- meaning 'before', 'front':   **'forstad, i 'forgårs**

21   UNSTRESSED SUFFIXES

-de, -else, -ig, -(n)ing, -isk, -me, -ske:

'højde, 'rettelse, 'rolig, 'regning, e'rotisk, 'sødme, 'sangerske

2 NOUNS

GENDER

22 GENDER

Danish nouns are either common gender (**en-** words) or neuter (**et-** words). The corresponding indefinite article (see **38**) is **en** or **et**, 'a(n)'. About 75 per cent of nouns are **en-** words and 25 per cent **et-** words.

Common gender *Indefinite*		Neuter *Indefinite*	
en mand a man	**en uge** a week	**et hus** a house	**et æble** an apple

Gender determines the form with end article (definite article) singular (see **38**):

Common gender *Definite*		Neuter *Definite*	
manden the man	**ugen** the week	**huset** the house	**æblet** the apple

Gender also determines the form of the adjective and some pronouns, as these agree in gender and number with nouns (see **44–49**, **68**, **74**):

en stor pige
a big girl

et stort hus
a big house

pigen er stor
the girl is big

huset er stort
the house is big

23 GENDER RULES

1 Common gender by meaning:
Personal names and nouns denoting human beings, animals, plants, trees, festivals and months and names of rivers are generally common gender:

en dreng, a boy; **en kone**, a wife; **en lærer**, a teacher; **en søster**, a sister; **en udlænding**, a foreigner; **en gås**, a goose; **en hund**, a dog; **en kat**, a cat; **en ko**, a cow; **en laks**, a salmon; **en rose**, a rose; **en birk**, a birch; **en eg**, an oak; **i julen**, at Christmas; **Themsen**, the Thames

Gender in proper nouns is usually shown by congruence with other words:

Bo er ung endnu.	Bo is still young.	(**ung** = common gender)
Januar var kold.	January was cold.	(**kold** = common gender)

cf. also

Danmark er ikke stort.   Denmark is not big.   (**stort** = neuter)

Exceptions: **et barn**, a child; **et bud**, a messenger; **et individ**, an individual; **et medlem**, a member; **et menneske**, a human being; **et vidne**, a witness; **et dyr**, an animal; **et egern**, a squirrel; **et føl**, a foal; **et kid**, a kid; **et får**, a sheep; **et lam**, a lamb; **et møl**, a moth; **et svin**, a pig; **et æsel**, a donkey; **et bær**, a berry; **et frø**, a seed; **et træ**, a tree; compounds in **-bær, -frø, -træ**.

2 Common gender by form, in nouns with the following suffixes:

-ance	**en ambulance**, an ambulance
-ans	**en substans**, a substance
-ant	**en repræsentant**, a representative
-de	**en bredde**, a breadth; **en længde**, a length
-dom	**en ejendom**, a property; **en sygdom**, an illness
-é	**en allé**, an avenue; **en café**, a café
-else	**en bevægelse**, a movement; **en skuffelse**, a disappointment

Exceptions: **et spøgelse**, a ghost; **et værelse**, a room.

-en	verbal nouns: **en formåen**, an ability; **en kunnen**, a capacity; **en væren**, (a) being; **en kommen og gåen**, coming and going
-ence	**en konference**, a conference
-ens	**en frekvens**, a frequency
-er	**en lærer**, a teacher
-hed	**en lejlighed**, a flat; **en tavshed**, a silence
-ik	**en grammatik**, a grammar
-ing	**en regning**, a bill; **en slægtning**, a relative; **en yndling**, a favourite
-ion	**en diskussion**, a discussion; **en situation**, a situation
-isme	**socialisme(n)**, socialism
-ør	**en direktør**, a director

For feminine suffixes see **23.7** below.

3 Neuter by meaning:
Nouns denoting substances, areas and localities, letters of the alphabet and nouns formed from other word classes (e.g. pronouns, interjections) are generally neuter:

(et) brød, bread; **glas**, glass; **jern**, iron; **kød**, meat; **papir**, paper; **snavs**, dirt; **vand**, water; **et kontinent**, a continent; **et sogn**, a parish; **et torv**, a square; **et langt i**, a long i; **et ja**, a yes; **jeget**, the ego

Exceptions: **en by**, a town; **en ø**, an island; **verden**, the world.

This also applies to proper names for geographical locations. In the case of countries the word **landet** is assumed:

Italien er dejligt om sommeren, Italy is lovely in summer; **det lille Danmark**, little Denmark

Exceptions: Notice that for towns the word **byen** is assumed: **(Byen) København er stor**.

4 Neuter by form, in nouns with the following suffixes:

-dømme   **et omdømme**, a reputation
-ed   **et hoved**, a head
-ende   **et udseende**, an appearance; **et velbefindende**, a well-being

Exceptions: These include people: **en gående**, a pedestrian; **en studerende**, a student.

-ri   **et bageri**, a bakery; **et batteri**, a battery
-um   **et gymnasium**, a sixth-form college; **et museum**, a museum

5 Suffixes where gender varies include:

-al   **en lineal**, a ruler; BUT: **et ideal**, an ideal
-ar   **en bibliotekar**, a librarian; BUT: **et eksemplar**, a copy
-at   usually neuter: **et certifikat**, a certificate; BUT: (people) **en demokrat**, a democrat
-ent   **en konsulent**, a consultant; BUT: **et departement**, a department
-i   **en industri**, an industry; BUT: **et parti**, a political party
-sel   **en trussel**, a threat; BUT: **et fængsel**, a prison
-skab   **en egenskab**, a quality; BUT: **et ægteskab**, a marriage

6 Compound nouns:
These nearly always take the gender of the second element in the compound:

en skole + **et køkken** → **et skolekøkken**, a school kitchen
et køkken + **en kniv** → **en køkkenkniv**, a kitchen knife

Exceptions:

et måltid, a meal, cf. **en tid**, a time

et bogstav, a letter of the alphabet, cf. **en stav**, a stave

7 Masculines and feminines:

Female suffixes include: **-esse**, **-inde**, **-ske**, **-øse**.

Matrimonial feminines are now rare: **baronesse**, baroness; **grevinde**, countess. Functional feminines in **-inde**, **-ske**, **-trice**, etc., have recently been curtailed as a result of political correctness: e.g. **lærer** and **lærerinde** → **lærer**, teacher; **nabo** and **naboerske** → **nabo**, neighbour.

Some gender-neutral terms have also been introduced recently: **folke-tingsmand** → **folketingsmedlem**, MP.

In a few cases where the gender is important these distinctions have been retained: **elsker** – **elskerinde**, lover; **samlever** – **samleverske**, co-habitee; **ven** – **veninde**, friend.

PLURALS

24   PLURALS AND DECLENSIONS

Danish nouns have three ways of forming regular plurals, by adding one of the following endings:

-(e)r, **-e**, **zero** (i.e. no plural ending)

About 75 per cent of nouns form the plural with **-(e)r**, 15 per cent in **-e**, and 10 per cent in **zero**. Note that nouns of both genders are found in all groups.

Nouns are grouped into the following three declensions according to their plural form.

First declension		*Second declension*	
-(e)r		**-e**	
en avis	**to aviser**	**en lærer**	**to lærere**
a newspaper	two newspapers	a teacher	two teachers
et værelse	**to værelser**	**et land**	**to lande**
a room	two rooms	a country	two countries

Third declension
zero plural

en fisk	**to fisk**
a fish	two fish
et lys	**to lys**
a light	two lights

25   PREDICTING PLURALS

Most plural forms can be predicted accurately from the form of the singular:

1 Structure and gender:
Monosyllabic common gender nouns ending in a consonant:

| add **-e** | **en hund** | **to hunde** |

Polysyllabic common gender nouns ending in **-e**:

| add **-r** | **en pige** | **to piger** |

Polysyllabic nouns ending in a consonant:

| add **-er** | **en regning** | **to regninger** |

Polysyllabic nouns with stress on the last syllable:

| add **-er** | **en appelsin** | **to appelsiner** |

2 Form of the final syllable:
Nouns ending in **-dom**:

| add **-me** | **en ejendom** | **to ejendomme** |

Nouns ending in unstressed **-er**:

| add **-e** | **en dansker** | **to danskere** |

Nouns ending in **-hed**:

| add **-er** | **en nyhed** | **to nyheder** |

Nouns ending in **-i**:

| add **-er** | **et vaskeri** | **to vaskerier** |

Nouns ending in **-ion**:

| add **-er** | **en station** | **to stationer** |

Nouns ending in **-skab**:

| add **-er** | **et venskab** | **to venskaber** |

Nouns ending in **-um** drop **-um** and add **-er**:

et museum   **to museer**

26   PLURALS IN -(E)R (EN GADE – GADER; ET BILLEDE – BILLEDER)

This group (known as the first declension) includes:

1 Almost all words ending in a vowel, including:

(a) Nouns ending in unstressed **-e** (which add **-r** in the plural):

en krone – kroner, crown; **en lampe – lamper**, lamp; **et menneske – mennesker**, human being; **et vindue – vinduer**, window

Exception: **et øje – øjne**, eye.

(b) Nouns ending in a stressed vowel:

en by – byer, town; **en ske – skeer**, spoon; **et træ – træer**, tree; **en ø – øer**, island; **en å – åer**, (small) river

Exception: **en sko – sko**, shoe.

2 Polysyllabic nouns, especially derivatives and loanwords, many of which have end stress:

en avis – aviser, newspaper; **en hilsen – hils(e)ner**, greeting; **et køkken – køk(ke)ner**, kitchen; **en måned – måneder**, month; **en paraply – paraplyer**, umbrella; **en tangent – tangenter**, tangent, piano key; **en telefon – telefoner**, telephone; **en turist – turister**, tourist

3 Polysyllabic nouns ending in **-hed, -skab**:

en enhed – enheder, unit; **et landskab – landskaber**, landscape

4 Many monosyllabic common gender nouns ending in a consonant:

en blomst – blomster, flower; **en flod – floder**, river; **en slægt – slægter**, family; **en ven – venner**, friend

27   PLURALS IN -E (EN DAG – DAGE; ET HUS – HUSE)

This group (known as the second declension) includes:

1 Many monosyllabic common gender nouns ending in a consonant (cf. **26.4** above):

en del – dele, part; **en dreng – drenge**, boy; **en fugl – fugle**, bird; **en krig – krige**, war; **en løgn – løgne**, lie; **en stol – stole**, chair; **en vej – veje**, road

2 Some monosyllabic neuter nouns:

et bord – borde, table; **et brev – breve**, letter; **et land – lande**, country

3 Nouns ending in unstressed **-er** (often denoting people):

en arbejder – arbejdere, worker; **en kunstner – kunstnere**, artist; **en lærer – lærere**, teacher; **en svensker – svenskere**, Swede; **en Århusianer – Århusianere**, inhabitant of Århus

4 Nouns ending in **-dom, -(n)ing**:

en ejendom – ejendomme, property; **en sygdom – sygdomme**, illness; **en udlænding – udlændinge**, foreigner; **en slægtning – slægtninge**, relative

28   ZERO-PLURAL (**EN SKO – SKO**; **ET ÅR – ÅR**)

This group (known as the third declension) includes:

1 Many monosyllabic neuter nouns:

et bær – bær, berry; **et dyr – dyr**, animal; **et glas – glas**, glass; **et kort – kort**, card; **et sprog – sprog**, language; **et tal – tal**, number; **et æg – æg**, egg; **et år – år**, year

2 Some polysyllabic neuter nouns ending in a consonant:

et forhold – forhold, relationship; **et forsøg – forsøg**, attempt

3 Some monosyllabic common gender nouns:

en fejl – fejl, mistake; **en mus – mus**, mouse; **en sko – sko**, shoe; **en sten – sten**, stone; **en ting – ting**, thing

4 Nouns (for temporary occupations) ending in **-ende**:

en rejsende – rejsende, traveller; **en studerende – studerende**, student

29   PLURALS WITH A VOWEL CHANGE (**EN TAND – TÆNDER**)

1 Vowel change + **er** (first declension):

A → Æ

en hovedstad	**hovedstæder**	capital
en kraft	**kræfter**	power
en nat	**nætter**	night
en tand	**tænder**	tooth

O → Ø

en bog	**bøger**	book
en bonde	**bønder**	farmer
en fod	**fødder**	feet
en ko	**køer**	cow

Å → Æ

en hånd	**hænder**	hand
en tå	**tæer**	toe

2 Vowel change + **e** (second declension):

A → Æ
en far (fader)	**fædre**	father

A → Ø
en datter	**døtre**	daughter

O → Ø
en bror (broder)	**brødre**	brother
en mor (moder)	**mødre**	mother

3 Vowel change + **zero** (third declension):

A → Æ
en mand	**mænd**	man

A → Ø
et barn	**børn**	child

Å → Æ
en gås	**gæs**	goose

30   PLURALS OF NOUNS IN -EL, -EN, -ER (EN SØSTER – SØSTRE)

Nouns ending in unstressed **-e** + **-l**, **-n**, **-r**, often drop the stem **-e-** in the plural, as well as the second part of any preceding double consonants.

1 **-er** plurals (first declension):

en aften	**aft(e)ner**	evening	**et eksempel**	**eksempler**	example
en kartoffel	**kartofler**	potato	**et køkken**	**køk(ke)ner**	kitchen

2 **-e** plurals (second declension):

en kælder	**kældre**	cellar	**et nummer**	**numre**	number
en søster	**søstre**	sister	**et register**	**registre**	register

31   NOUNS DOUBLING THE FINAL CONSONANT

Nouns ending in a short stressed vowel double the following consonant when adding the plural ending (or end article) (see also **2**):

en bus	**busser**	bus
en butik	**butikker**	shop
en hat	**hatte**	hat
et hotel	**hoteller**	hotel
en ven	**venner**	friend
en væg	**vægge**	wall
en sygdom	**sygdomme**	illness

32 PLURALS OF LOANWORDS

1 Loanwords from Latin and Italian:
These tend to retain the plural form from their original language:

et faktum	fakta	fact
et visum	visa	visa

But note the adaptation to Danish inflexions in:

et drama	dramaer	drama
en kollega	kolleg(a)er	colleague
en cello	celloer	cello
et konto	konti/kontoer	account
et gymnasium	gymnasier	sixth-form college
et museum	museer	museum
et centrum	centrer/centrum(m)er	centre
et kursus	kurser/kursus	course

2 Loans from English:

(a) Some loans retain their plural in **-s** at least as an alternative to the Danish plural form:

en check – check(s); en cowboy – cowboys/cowboyer; en fan – fans; et foto – fotos/fotoer; en/et gag – gags; en jumper – jumpers/ jumpere; et party – parties/partyer

(b) Notice, however, adaptation to Danish inflexion in:

en baby – babyer; en shop – shopper; en weekend – weekender en computer – computere; en sweater – sweatere en film – film; et job – job; et point – point

(c) Some nouns occurring in the plural or collective only have a form in **-s**:

conflakes, jeans, odds, shorts

33 COUNT AND NON-COUNT NOUNS

1 Count nouns are nouns that have both a singular and a plural form. They represent individual entities and can be preceded by an indefinite article and by numerals.

en pige	to piger	en sko	to sko
a girl	two girls	a shoe	two shoes

Count nouns are often words for concrete entities and creatures. Some abstract nouns are count nouns: **evne**, ability; **spørgsmål**, question.

Non-count nouns are only found in the singular form:

kaffe (-n)   **mælk (-en)**   **vand (-et)**
coffee   milk   water

2 Non-count nouns are often words for materials and substances.
Most abstract nouns are non-count nouns: **kedsomhed**, boredom; **lykke**,
happiness.

Note: A few nouns have both a count plural and a collective plural form:

	Count plural	*Collective plural*
en mand	**mænd**	**mand**

e.g. **en gruppe på 10 mand**, a group of ten men
en øl   **øller** (bottles of beer)   **øl** (types of beer)
e.g. **Han kom med tre øller**. He arrived with three bottles of beer.

34   NOUNS WITH NO PLURAL FORM

These include:

1 Verbal nouns ending in **-en**:	**grublen**, brooding; **hensynstagen**, consideration. See also **23.2**.
2 Abstract nouns:	**ansvar**, responsibility; **fattigdom**, poverty
3 Substances and materials:	**kød**, meat; **sne**, snow; **vand**, water

Note: Plurals of nouns of this kind are used to indicate types or makes, 'kinds of': **teer**, teas; **vine**, wines.

4 Nouns indicating quantity:	**fire kilo ost**, four kilos of cheese **tre liter mælk**, three litres of milk

35   NOUNS WITH NO SINGULAR FORM

These include:

1 Articles of clothing:	**bukser**, trousers; **trusser**, knickers; **tøj**, clothes
2 Other collectives:	**briller**, glasses; **penge**, money; **søskende**, brothers and sisters

36   DIFFERENCES IN NUMBER

1 Singular in English, plural in Danish:

kontanter, cash; **møbler**, furniture; **oplysninger**, information; **penge**,
money; **råd**, advice

Notice: **møbler**, furniture – **et møbel**, a piece of furniture; **nyheder**, news
– **en nyhed**, a piece of news; **råd**, advice – **et råd**, a piece of advice.

2 Plural in English, singular in Danish:

indhold, contents; **løn**, wages; **saks**, pair of scissors; **statistik** (and others in **-ik**), statistics; **trappe**, stairs

THE GENITIVE

37   GENITIVES

1 The genitive ending **-s** is added to the indefinite or definite singular or to the indefinite or definite plural form:

en drengs hund
a boy's dog

drengens hund
the boy's dog

et barns værelse
a child's room

barnets værelse
the child's room

drenges hunde
boys' dogs

drengenes hunde
the boys' dogs

børns værelser
children's rooms

børnenes værelser
the children's rooms

2 Proper nouns also take the genitive **-s**: **Torbens kat**, Torben's cat; **Grundtvigs salmer**, Grundtvig's hymns; **Danmarks hovedstad**, the capital of Denmark.

3 If a noun ends in **-s**, **-x** or **-z** in the singular several alternatives are possible:

Jens's lejlighed or **Jens' lejlighed** or **Jenses lejlighed** (Jens' flat)
Marx's or **Marx' bøger** (Marx's books)

With inanimate nouns it is best to use a prepositional phrase instead:

vores hus'/hus's tag → **taget på vores hus**   the roof of our house

4 Some old genitive case endings remain in set phrases after **til**:

til havs, by sea; **til sengs**, to bed. See also **124**.

5 The genitive **-s** is placed on the last word of the noun phrase. This is known as the 'group genitive':

Herman Bangs romaner   the novels of Herman Bang
en af mine venners far   the father of one of my friends

6 Notice the different use of the definite article in English and Danish:

the end of winter   ← →   **vinterens afslutning**, i.e. *lit.* the winter's end
definite   no article   definite no article
article   article

Nouns following a genitive never take an end article in Danish.

7 As in the last example, the **-s** genitive often corresponds to English 'of-constructions' (see also **131**):

gårdens ejer	the owner of the farm
dronning Margrethes liv	the life of Queen Margrethe
Danmarks statsminister	the Prime Minister of Denmark
forårets første dag	the first day of spring

8 The **-s** genitive has two special uses:

- in surnames, denoting 'family' or 'shop':

  hos Olsens, at the Olsens'
  Vi køber fisk hos Hansens.
  We buy fish at Hansen's.

- as a genitive of measurement:

  et fyrreminutters tv-program
  a 40-minute TV programme
  en 75 centiliters vinflaske
  a 75-centilitre wine bottle

ARTICLES

38   ARTICLES – FORM

1 The indefinite article (corresponding to English 'a', 'an') is in Danish either **en** or **et**. The end (definite) article (corresponding to English 'the'), which may be **-(e)n** or **-(e)t**, is added as a suffix to the end of the noun, either to its dictionary form or to its inflected form:

Singular

Indefinite (**en/et**)		*Definite (end article)* (**-(e)n/-(e)t**)	
en mand	a man	**manden**	the man
en kvinde	a woman	**kvinden**	the woman
et hus	a house	**huset**	the house
et æble	an apple	**æblet**	the apple

Plural (both genders) (**-(e)ne**)
-(e)r plural

aviser	newspapers	**aviserne**	the newspapers
æbler	apples	**æblerne**	the apples

-e plural

heste	horses	**hestene**	the horses

zero plural

mænd	men	**mændene**	the men

2 Rules for the end article singular:

(a) Add **-n**, **-t** when the noun ends in unstressed **-e**:

en uge – **ugen**, week   **et billede** – **billedet**, picture

(b) When the noun ends in another vowel or stressed **-e (-é)**, add **-en**, **-et**:

en by – **byen**, town   **et strå** – **strået**, straw
en café – **cafeen**, café   **et træ** – **træet**, tree

3 When the noun ends in a consonant (but cf. **4**, **5**), add **-en**, **-et**:

en hånd – **hånden**, hand   **et barn** – **barnet**, child

4 When the noun ends in unstressed **e** + **l**, **n**, **r**, drop the **-e-** of the stem and add **-en**, **-et**:

titel – **titlen**, title   **teater** – **teatret**, theatre

But many of these nouns possess alternative definite forms with or without the vowel:

en aften – **aft(e)nen**, evening   **et køkken** – **køk(ke)net**, kitchen

5 Nouns in **-um** drop the **-um** before adding the end article:

et museum – **museet**, museum

6 After a short stressed vowel the final consonant is doubled before adding the end article (see **2**):

en ven – **vennen**, friend   **et hotel** – **hotellet**, hotel

7 The end article plural is usually **-ne**:

byer – **byerne**, towns   **stole** – **stolene**, chairs
gader – **gaderne**, streets   **borde** – **bordene**, tables

But notice that nouns in **-ere** drop the final **-e**: **danskere** – **danskerne**, Danes.

8 If the noun has a **zero** plural the end article plural is **-ene**:

børn – **børnene**, children   **sko** – **skoene**, shoes
dyr – **dyrene**, animals   **år** – **årene**, years

39   ARTICLE USE – INTRODUCTION

1 In most cases the same principle applies to the use of articles in Danish as in English, namely that when a noun refers anaphorically to a previously mentioned occurrence (when it is a familiar idea or has unique reference), it takes a definite (end) article, whilst a noun for an entity or concept not

previously mentioned (non-unique reference) takes an indefinite article. In short, the first time a noun appears it is likely to be in the indefinite form, the next time it will be definite:

De havde købt *et nyt hus*. *Huset* lå ved *en sø*. *Søen* var lille, men dyb.

←——————   ←——————
1ˢᵗ time   next time   1ˢᵗ time next time

They had bought a new house. The house lay by a lake. The lake was small but deep.

2   Concepts that are associated semantically with a previously mentioned noun (e.g. whole-part or type-example), and those that are obvious to everyone, use the definite form:

Han har *en cykel*, men *gearet* virker ikke.

←——————————
first time   associated

He has a bike but the gear doesn't work.

Jeg købte forskellige *blomster*, men *roserne* visnede hurtigt.

←——————————
first time   associated

I bought different flowers, but the roses withered quickly.

Vejret var fint. Solen skinnede. Så jeg vaskede *bilen*.
obvious   obvious   obvious

The weather was fine. The sun was shining. So I washed the car.

3   However, in some cases, outlined in **40–43** below, the languages differ in their use of the articles.

40   ARTICLE USE – END ARTICLE IN DANISH, NO ARTICLE IN ENGLISH

1 Abstract nouns and nouns in a generic sense:

tilbage til *naturen*	back to nature
livet* efter *døden	life after death
***Danskerne* drikker meget øl.**	Danes drink a lot of beer.

This applies especially to nouns depicting human life and thought: **arbejdet**, work; **krigen**, war; **kærligheden**, love.

2 Many proverbs:

***Historien* gentager sig.**	History repeats itself.
Sådan er *livet*.	That's life.

3 Some idiomatic phrases for location and time:

Han er i byen/tager til byen.   He's in town/going to town.
But: **Hun går i kirke/i skole/på arbejde.**   She goes to church/school/
                                        work.

om vinteren/mandagen   in winter/on Mondays
i julen/påsken   at Christmas/Easter

41 ARTICLE USE – NO ARTICLE IN DANISH, DEFINITE ARTICLE IN ENGLISH

1 After certain words:

Samme aften kom vi hjem.   The same evening we arrived home.
Næste dag var vejret dejligt. The next day the weather was beautiful.
De bor på øverste etage.   They live on the top floor.

Note: **den næste måned**, the following month; **det næste år**, the following year.

2 In some idiomatic phrases:

De hører radio.   They listen to the radio.
Bodil spiller klaver/violin. Bodil plays the piano/violin.
Mor læser avis.   Mother is reading the paper.
Hun er datter af en præst.   She is the daughter of a vicar.

3 With proper nouns:

Vi spiste frokost hos Olsens.   We had lunch at the Olsens'.

42 ARTICLE USE – NO ARTICLE IN DANISH, INDEFINITE ARTICLE IN ENGLISH

With nouns denoting nationality, profession, religion or political beliefs:

Marie er dansker/læge/katolik/socialist.
Marie is a Dane/a doctor/a Catholic/a socialist.

Hun arbejder som læge/læser til lærer.
She is working as a doctor/is studying to become a teacher.

Notice that if the noun is qualified by an attributive adjective or relative clause, the indefinite article must be added:

Hun er en dygtig læge.   She is a skilled doctor.
Han er en dansker der elsker   He is a Dane who likes good
  god mad.   food.

In some cases a figurative use of the noun is indicated by the use of the indefinite article. Compare:

Coco var klovn. Coco was a clown (literal = occupation).

Søren var en klovn. Søren was a clown (figurative = was a fool).

43   ARTICLE USE – END ARTICLE IN DANISH, POSSESSIVE PRONOUN IN ENGLISH

With nouns denoting parts of the body and clothing where possession is obvious, Danish prefers the end article to the possessive pronoun:

Jeg har ondt i armen/benet/hånden/maven.
I have a pain in my arm/leg/hand/stomach.

Erik stak hånden i lommen.
Erik put his hand in his pocket.

3 ADJECTIVES

Danish adjectives inflect. In the indefinite declension they agree with the noun in gender (singular only) and number both attributively and predicatively. They also add inflexional endings in the definite declension.

INDEFINITE FORMS

	Common gender	Neuter	Plural
Attributive	**en stor⊗ bil**	**et stor*t* hus**	**store biler/huse**
	a big car	a big house	big cars/houses
	god⊗ mad	**varm*t* vand**	**smukk*e* piger**
	good food	hot water	beautiful girls
Predicative	**bilen er stor⊗**	**huset er stor*t***	**bilerne/husene er store**
	the car is big	the house is big	the cars/houses are big

DEFINITE FORMS

	den stor*e* bil	**det stor*e* hus**	**de stor*e* biler/huse**
	the big car	the big house	the big cars/houses
	min stor*e* bil	**mit stor*e* hus**	**mine stor*e* biler/huse**
	my big car	my big house	my big cars/houses

INDEFINITE DECLENSION

45 INDEFINITE FORM – REGULAR

1 Main rule:

Common gender	Neuter	Plural
zero (⊗)	**+ t**	**+ e**
en fin have	**et fint hus**	**fine haver/huse**
a fine garden	a fine house	fine gardens/houses
en rolig by	**et roligt sted**	**rolige byer/steder**
a quiet town	a quiet place	quiet towns/places

2 Note that some monosyllabic adjectives with a long vowel + consonant in the common gender form shorten the vowel in the pronunciation of the neuter form: **god** [go'ð] – **godt** [gɔd].

Other examples of neuter forms with a short vowel: **dødt**, dead; **hvidt**, white; **fedt**, fatty; **fladt**, flat; **rødt**, red; **sødt**, sweet; **vådt**, wet.

3 Adjectives following the main rule include:

(a) many monosyllabic adjectives ending in a consonant or consonant group:

dyb, deep; **høj**, high, tall; **kold**, cold; **mørk**, dark; **varm**, hot, warm

(b) polysyllabic adjectives ending in **-al, -bar, -el, -ig, -iv, -ær, -(i)øs**:

social, social; **dyrebar**, expensive; **kontroversiel**, controversial; **dygtig**, capable; **naiv**, naive; **vulgær**, vulgar; **seriøs**, serious

46   INDEFINITE FORM – NEUTER SAME AS COMMON GENDER

In the following cases the neuter form has no special ending:

1 Adjectives ending in **-(i)sk**:

Common gender	*Neuter*	*Plural*
en dansk⊗ forfatter	**et dansk⊗ skib**	**dansk*e* forfattere/skibe**
a Danish writer	a Danish ship	Danish writers/ships

Other examples: **automatisk**, automatic; **elektrisk**, electrical; **fynsk**, of Fyn; **økonomisk**, economic.

This group includes most adjectives denoting nationality or geographical location: **amerikansk**, American; **engelsk**, English; **fransk**, French; **tysk**, German.

In some adjectives ending in **-sk** the neuter **-t** ending is optional: **besk(t)**, bitter; **fersk(t)**, fresh.

2 Adjectives with stems already ending in **-t**:

en sort⊗ kat	**et sort⊗ hul**	**sort*e* katte/huller**
a black cat	a black hole	black cats/holes

Other examples: **flot**, posh; **kort**, short; **let**, light; **mæt**, replete; **smart**, smart; **tæt**, close.

(a) This group includes many polysyllabic loans ending in **-t, -at, -ant, -ent**:

abstrakt, privat, tolerant, konsekvent

(b) A few adjectives ending in a vowel + **d** have no special neuter form: **fremmed**, foreign; **glad**, happy; **ked**, bored; **lad**, lazy.

(c) A few adjectives ending in a consonant + **d** where the **d** is pronounced [d] have no special neuter form: **absurd**, absurd; **lærd**, learned.

47   VARIATIONS IN PLURAL/DEFINITE

In the following cases the plural form varies from the main rule given in **44** above, i.e. it does not simply add **-e-**:

1 Adjectives ending in **-el**, **-en**, **-er** drop the **-e-** of the stem before adding the plural or definite ending **-e:**

Common gender	Neuter	Plural
en gammel kone	**et gammelt hus**	**gamle koner/huse**
an old woman	an old house	old women/houses

Compare the definite forms:

den gamle kone	**det gamle hus**	**de gamle koner/huse**
the old woman	the old house	the old women/houses

This group includes: **bitter**, bitter; **doven**, idle; **lækker**, delicious; **mager**, thin; **moden**, ripe; **rusten**, rusty; **sikker**, sure; **simpel**, simple; **voksen**, adult; **ædel**, noble; **åben**, open.

It also includes loanwords in **-abel**, **-ibel**: **diskutabel**, debatable; **flexibel**, flexible.

2 Adjectives in **-et** change the **-t** to a **-d** before adding the plural/definite ending **-e:**

en blomstret⊗ vest	**et blomstret⊗ forklæde**	**blomstre*de* gardiner**
a flowery waistcoat	a flowery pinafore	flowery curtains

This group includes: **broget**, multicoloured, and many past participles, e.g. **elsket**, loved; **forlovet**, engaged; **malet**, painted; **pakket**, packed; **repareret**, repaired; **slukket**, extinguished; **ternet**, checked.

48   INDEFINITE FORM – SPECIAL CASES

1 The adjective **lille**:

Common gender	Neuter	Plural
en lille⊗ pige	**et lille⊗ barn**	**små piger/børn**
	(no **-t** ending)	(new stem in plural)
a small girl	a small child	small girls/children

Note also the definite forms:

den lille⊗ pige	**det lille⊗ barn**	**de *små* piger/børn**
the small girl	the small child	the small girls/children

2 Adjectives ending in **-å**:

en blå⊗ (grå⊗) skjorte   **et blå*t* (grå*t*) halstørklæde**   **blå⊗ (grå⊗) bukser**
                                                                  (no **-e** in plural)
a blue (grey) shirt   a blue (grey) scarf   blue (grey) trousers

3 Adjectives ending in **-v**:

en grov⊗ stemme   **et gro*ft* brød**   **grov*e* brædder**
                        (v → f)
a coarse voice   a coarse loaf   coarse boards

Also: **stiv – stift – stive**, stiff.

4 The past participle forms of some strong verbs – when used attributively – are usually found in the neuter form even with common gender
nouns: **en stjålet** (or **stjålen**) **cykel**, a stolen bike; **en maskinskrevet** (or
maskinskreven) **meddelelse**, a typewritten message. The common gender
form in such cases is now considered formal.

49   ADJECTIVES DOUBLING THE FINAL CONSONANT IN THE PLURAL

Adjectives ending in a short stressed vowel plus a single consonant double
the final consonant when adding the plural/definite ending in **-e**:

en tom æske   **et tomt hus**   **tomme tønder**
an empty box   an empty house   empty barrels

Many adjectives do this, e.g. **flot**, posh; **grim**, ugly; **grøn**, green; **let**, easy,
light; **mæt**, replete; **slem**, nasty; **smuk**, pretty; **tom**, empty; **træt**, tired; **tyk**,
fat; **tør**, dry.
See also **31**.

50   INDECLINABLE ADJECTIVES

Some adjectives add no endings for either neuter or plural. These include
the following groups:

1 Adjectives ending in **-e**:

en moderne⊗ bil   **et moderne⊗ hus**   **moderne⊗ mennesker**
a modern car   a modern house   modern people

This group includes: **bange**, afraid; **lige**, equal; **stille**, calm; **øde**, deserted,
and includes some ordinal numbers and present participles: **tredje**, third;
fjerde, fourth; **glimrende**, brilliant; **irriterende**, irritating; **rasende**, furious.

2 Many adjectives ending in a stressed vowel:

en snu⊗ mand   **et snu⊗ vidne**   **snu⊗ forretningsmænd**
a wily man   a wily witness   wily businessmen

This group includes: **kry**, cocky; **sky**, shy; **tro**, faithful; **ædru**, sober.

Exceptions: **fri – frit – fri(e)**, free; **ny – nyt – ny(e)**, new.

3 Adjectives ending in **-s**:

en fælles⊗ sag   **et fælles⊗ projekt**   **fælles⊗ venner**
a common cause   a joint project   mutual friends

This group includes: **afsides**, remote; **ens**, identical; **gammeldags**, old-fashioned; **indbyrdes**, mutual; **stakkels**, poor; **tilfreds**, contented.

Exceptions: Adjectives ending in a long vowel + **s**: **tavs – tavst – tavse**, silent. Also: **løs**, loose; **nervøs**, nervous.

4 Some other adjectives, often used only predicatively, do not inflect:

Det er *forkert/slut*.   It is wrong/finished.
Det er *værd* at lægge mærke til.   It is worth noticing.

51   INDEFINITE CONSTRUCTIONS

The indefinite noun phrase (in this case: indefinite premodifier + adjective + noun, e.g. **en** + **ny** + **bil**) usually expresses something general and non-specific. The following indefinite constructions are found:

Common gender	*Neuter*	*Plural*
god mad	**fint vejr**	**lige veje** (no premodifier)
good food	fine weather	straight roads
en ny bil	**et nyt hus**	**to nye biler/huse**
a new car	a new house	two new cars/houses
ikke nogen sjov film	**noget varmt brød**	**nogle saftige æbler**
not a funny film	some hot bread	some juicy apples
ikke nogen god idé	**ikke noget nyt forslag**	**ikke nogen gode idéer**
no good idea	no new proposal	no good ideas
sådan en dyr jakke	**sådan et stærkt tov**	**sådan nogle store sko**
an expensive jacket like that	a strong rope like that	big shoes like that
sikken varme	**sikket vejr**	**sikke farver**
what a heat	what weather	what colours
sikke(n) en kold blæst	**sikken et fint vejr**	**sikke nogle mørke skyer**
what a cold wind	what beautiful weather	what dark clouds

Common gender	*Neuter*	*Plural*
hvilken ung mand	**hvilket stort slot**	**hvilke nye møbler**
what young man	what big castle	what new furniture
–		**mange onde gerninger**
		many evil deeds
–	–	**alle unge mennesker**
		all young people

52   AGREEMENT AND LACK OF AGREEMENT

1 Usually adjectives agree with the noun they qualify:

Common gender	*Neuter*	*Plural*
Bilen er stor⊗.	**Huset er stort.**	**Æblerne er gode.**
The car is big.	The house is big.	The apples are good.

2 Some abstract nouns formed from verbs do, however, require the neuter form of the adjective even when they are common gender:

Rygning er skadeligt.   (rygning-en)   **Det er skadeligt at ryge.**
Smoking is harmful.   It is harmful to smoke.

Svømning er dejligt.   (svømning-en)   **Det er dejligt at svømme.**
Swimming is lovely.   It is lovely to swim.

This also applies to infinitive phrases that are used as subject:

At svømme er dejligt.   Swimming is lovely.

3 Nouns used in a general, abstract or collective sense normally require the neuter form of the adjective:

Fisk er dyrt.   (fisk-en)   Fish is expensive.
Frugt er sundt.   (frugt-en)   Fruit is healthy.

Cf. **Det er dyrt at købe fisk.**   **Det er sundt at spise frugt.**
It is expensive to buy fish.   Eating fruit is healthy.

4 Past participle agreement:
Past participles after **være/blive** usually agree with a plural subject:

Bilerne er røde/importerede.   The cars are red/imported.
ADJECTIVE/PAST PARTICIPLE

But past participles of some verbs only agree with the subject when depicting a state (adjectival), and take the neuter form when used to emphasise an action (verbal) in which case they are less closely linked to the subject (see also **92.3**):

State	*Action*
Stolene er male*de*.	**Stolene er male*t*.**
The chairs are painted.	The chairs are (have been) painted.
(as opposed to 'unpainted')	(Watch out for the wet paint!)

Examples with a plural subject:

Priserne er fald*et*.	Prices have fallen.
De var drag*et* bort.	They had left.
Syv dage er gå*et*.	A week has passed.
Ti demonstranter blev arrester*et*.	Ten demonstrators were arrested.
Alle eleverne var saml*et*.	All the pupils had assembled.

5 In a few cases the inherent sense of the subject (plural) may override
the strict grammatical number (singular):

Man var uenig*e*.	They had a difference of opinion.
Brudeparret var lykkelig*e*/lykkelig*t*.	The bridal couple were happy.

DEFINITE DECLENSION

53 DEFINITE CONSTRUCTIONS

There are three types of definite construction of adjective + noun:

Common gender	*Neuter*	*Plural*

TYPE 1 After the front articles **den**, **det**, **de**, the demonstratives **den**,
det, **de** and **denne**, **dette**, **disse**:

den røde dør	**det røde tag**	**de røde vægge**
the red door	the red roof	the red walls
denne nye båd	**dette nye skib**	**disse nye færger**
this new boat	this new ship	these new ferries

These are the most frequent uses of the definite declension.

TYPE 2 After genitives and possessive pronouns:

Karens store gård	**familiens fattige hjem**	**pigens gamle sko**
Karen's big farm	the family's poor home	the girl's old shoes
min varme jakke	**mit varme tørklæde**	**mine varme strømper**
my warm jacket	my warm scarf	my warm socks
vores grønne vase	**vores hvide spisebord**	**vores sorte stole**
our green vase	our white dining table	our black chairs

Exception: After a genitive or possessive pronoun the adjective **egen** is inflected
according to the indefinite declension:

Mors egen lille Niels	Mum's own little Niels
Han har sit eget hus.	He has his own house.

TYPE 3 With no article preceding the adjective + noun:

Kære ven!   **ovennævnte brev**   **omtalte forfattere**
Dear friend!   the above-mentioned letter   the aforementioned authors

Notes:

1 When an adjective is used before a noun in the definite, the end (definite) article is replaced by a front article **den**, **det**, **de**:

mand*en*   →   *den* **gamle mand**
the man   the old man

2 The definite form of the adjective is identical to the plural form in nearly all cases, i.e. **-e** is added to the basic form:

en grøn skov	**grønne skove**	**den grønne skov**	**de grønne skove**
a green forest	green forests	the green forest	the green forests

3 Type 3 above is found in some names of people and places: **lille Erik**, **Store Kongensgade**, **Gamle Carlsberg**, **Vestre Fængsel** and in officialese.

It is also found with the words **første**, **sidste**, **forrige**, **næste**, **samme**: **første gang**, the first time; **sidste forestilling**, the final performance; **forrige uge**, last week; **næste fredag**, next Friday; **samme alder**, the same age.

4 With the words **hele** and **selve** an end article is added to the noun: **hele tiden**, the whole time:

Selve lejligheden er god, men beliggenheden er dårlig. The flat itself is fine, but its location is poor.

54   ADJECTIVAL NOUNS

1 There are three cases in which adjectives are used as nouns:

(a) when the noun is omitted in order to avoid repetition:

Han foretrækker dansk mad fremfor fremmed (mad).
He prefers Danish food to foreign food.

(b) when a noun that is not mentioned is understood (these are what are usually known as adjectival nouns):

De unge forstår ikke de gamle. (mennesker is understood after both **unge** and **gamle)**
Young people do not understand old people.

(c) independent use of the adjective with no noun understood:

Valget stod mellem grønt og blåt.
The choice was between green and blue.

2 Danish uses adjectival nouns in the definite plural in the same way as English:

de arbejdsløse, the unemployed; **de fattige**, the poor; **de rige**, the rich; **de syge**, the sick; **de sårede**, the wounded; **de unges verden**, the world of the young

Notice from this last example that adjectival nouns have a (noun) genitive in **-s**:

de retfærdiges søvn　　　　　　the sleep of the just

3 Danish also uses the common gender indefinite adjective as a noun:

en fremmed, a stranger; **en gal**, a madman; **en lille**, a little child; **en lærd**, a scholar; **en nyfødt**, a new-born baby; **en sagkyndig**, an expert; **en voksen**, an adult

4 In a few cases Danish uses the neuter definite form of the adjective nominally:

Det er det fine ved ham.　　　That's the nice thing about him.
i det fri　　　　　　　　　　　in the open air

Note: This also applies to the superlative: **gøre sit bedste**, do one's best.

5 In many cases where Danish has a definite adjectival noun, English has a count noun:

den myrdede, the murder victim; **den uskyldige**, the innocent person; **de kongelige**, the royals; **de overlevende**, the survivors; **de rejsende**, the travellers

6 Neuter adjectival nouns in Danish may correspond to abstract nouns or concepts in English:

det gode, good(ness); **det passende**, what is suitable

7 In a few cases Danish also uses the singular definite form of the adjective without an article as a noun to denote people and numbered entities (cf. **53**, Type 3):

elskede, my love; **undertegnede**, the undersigned

Jeg bor på fjerde (sal).　　　　I live on the fourth (floor).
Frederik skal op i sjette (klasse).　Frederik is going into the sixth class.

55　'THE ENGLISH' AND OTHER NATIONALITY WORDS

Whereas English often employs adjectival nouns such as 'the English', 'the French' to express nationality, Danish prefers proper nouns, e.g.

englænderne, franskmændene. Some frequent nationality words are listed below.

Country	Adjective	Inhabitant
Amerika (De Forenede Stater)	amerikansk	amerikaner-e
Danmark	dansk	dansker-e
England (Storbritannien)	engelsk (britisk)	englænder-e (briter-e)
Europa	europæisk	europæer-e
Finland	finsk	finne-r
Frankrig	fransk	franskmand, -mænd
Grækenland	græsk	græker-e
Holland	hollandsk	hollænder-e
Irland	irsk	irer-e, irlænder-e
Island	islandsk	islænding-e
Italien	italiensk	italiener-e
Japan	japansk	japaner-e
Kina	kinesisk	kineser-e
Litauen	litauisk	litauer-e
Norge	norsk	nordmand, -mænd
Rusland	russisk	russer-e
Spanien	spansk	spanier-e, spaniol-er
Sverige	svensk	svensker-e
Tyskland	tysk	tysker-e

COMPARISON

56 COMPARISON – INTRODUCTION

The comparative form of the adjective in **-(e)re** is indeclinable, i.e. the adjective has the same form for definite and indefinite. Note, however, that the superlative in **-(e)st** has two forms (**-(e)st/-(e)ste**, see **62**).

1 Comparison implies that:

- two objects or circumstances are contrasted:

  Søren er højere end Erik. Søren is taller than Erik.

- one object or circumstance is contrasted with itself at a different juncture:

  Det er mere overskyet i dag. It is more overcast today.

2 There are four different methods of comparison:

(a) Add **-ere**, **-est** to the positive (basic) form:

pæn – pænere – pænest   See **57**.

(b) Change the stem vowel of the positive form and add **-re, -(e)st**:

ung – yngre – yngst   See **58**.

(c) Irregular comparison (change of stem):

god – bedre – bedst   See **59**.

(d) Comparison with **mere, mest** and the positive form:

snavset – mere snavset – mest snavset   See **60**.

57   COMPARISON WITH **-ERE, -EST**

1 The most common method of showing comparison is to add **-ere** and **-est** to the adjective:

Positive	*Comparative*	*Superlative*
glad	**glad***ere*	**glad***est*
happy	happier	happiest

Most adjectives compare this way, including: **dyb**, deep; **dyr**, expensive; **fin**, fine; **høj**, high; **hård**, hard; **kold**, cold; **kort**, short; **lav**, low; **lys**, light; **mørk**, dark; **ny**, new; **pæn**, beautiful; **sjov**, fun; **tung**, heavy; **tynd**, thin.

2 Adjectives ending in a short stressed vowel plus a consonant often double the final consonant before adding the comparative and superlative endings (cf. **49**):

smuk	**smukkere**	**smukkest**
beautiful	more beautiful	most beautiful

See also **31**.

3 Adjectives ending in **-en, -el, -er** drop the **-e-** of the stem before adding the comparative and superlative endings:

sikker	**sikrere**	**sikrest**
safe	safer	safest

See also **30**.

4 **Nær** has deviant forms:

nær	**nærmere**	**nærmest**
close	closer	closest

5 A few adjectives (often ending in **-ig** and **-som**) add **-ere** but **-st** (and not **-est**) to the positive form:

kedelig	**kedeligere**	**kedeligst**
boring	more boring	most boring
morsom	**morsommere**	**morsomst**
funny	funnier	funniest

Others: **farlig**, dangerous; **fattig**, poor; **langsom**, slow; **voldsom**, violent.

58   COMPARISON WITH VOWEL CHANGE AND -(E)RE, -(E)ST

Only four adjectives modify the root vowel before adding the comparative or superlative ending:

Positive	Comparative	Superlative	
få	**færre**	**færrest**	few
lang	**længere**	**længst**	long
stor	**større**	**størst**	big
ung	**yngre**	**yngst**	young

59   IRREGULAR COMPARISON

1 The following adjectives change their stem in the comparative and superlative:

Positive	Comparative	Superlative	
dårlig, slem	**værre**	**værst**	bad
gammel	**ældre**	**ældst**	old
god	**bedre**	**bedst**	good
lidt, lille	**mindre**	**mindst**	small
mange	**flere**	**flest**	many
meget (megen)	**mere**	**mest**	much

2 **Værre, værst** often indicate 'more of a bad quality': **Hendes dårlige ben er blevet værre**, Her bad leg has got worse (i.e. it was bad to begin with); whereas **dårligere, dårligest** often indicate less of a good quality: **Kartoflerne er blevet dårligere i år**, The potatoes have got worse this year (i.e. they may have been good last year).

3 **Flere, flest** are plural forms used with count nouns: **Vi købte flere bøger**, We bought more books; whereas **mere, mest** are singular forms used with non-count nouns: **Vil du have mere øl?**, Would you like some more beer?

For count/non-count nouns see **33**.

60   COMPARISON WITH **MERE, MEST**

This group includes a number of different types:

1 Present and past participles and most longer adjectives:

Positive	*Comparative*	*Superlative*
spændende	**mere spændende**	**mest spændende**
exciting	more exciting	most exciting
velkendt	**mere velkendt**	**mest velkendt**
well-known	more well-known	most well-known

2 Adjectives ending in **-et**:

interesseret	**mere interesseret**	**mest interesseret**
interested	more interested	most interested

Others: **forvirret**, confused; **skuffet**, disappointed; **snavset**, dirty; **tosset**, foolish.

3 All adjectives ending in **-isk** and most ending in **-sk**:

praktisk	**mere praktisk**	**mest praktisk**
practical	more practical	most practical

Others: **dansk**, Danish; **fantastisk**, fantastic; **humoristisk**, humorous; **jordisk**, earthly; **musikalsk**, musical; **realistisk**, realistic.

Exceptions: **barsk**, harsh; **besk**, bitter; **fersk**, fresh; **frisk**, fresh, go according to the main rule with the endings **-ere**, **-est**.

4 Some adjectives ending in **-en**:

sulten	**mere sulten**	**mest sulten**
hungry	more hungry	most hungry

Others: **voksen**, adult; **vågen**, awake; **åben**, open.

5 Some adjectives ending in unstressed **-e** and short adjectives ending in a vowel:

bange	**mere bange**	**mest bange**
afraid	more afraid	most afraid

Others: **grå**, grey; **lige**, similar; **stille**, peaceful; **ædru**, sober.

6 Some loanwords:

desperat	**mere desperat**	**mest desperat**
desperate	more desperate	most desperate

61   SIMILARITY, DISSIMILARITY AND REINFORCEMENT

There are a number of ways of expressing similarity, dissimilarity and reinforcement other than by using comparison (cf. **57–60** above):

1 Similarity:

lige så + adj + **som**	**Hun var lige så venlig som hun var smuk.**
as ... as	She was as friendly as she was beautiful.
samme + noun + **som**	**De taler samme dialekt som os.**
the same ... as	They speak the same dialect as us.
ligne	**Han ligner sin far.**
be/look like	He is/looks like his father.

2 Dissimilarity:

ikke så + adj + **som**	**Hun var ikke så rig som Greta Garbo.**
not as ... as	She wasn't as rich as Greta Garbo.

The particle **end** is often used with comparatives:

Min bror er stærkere end din.   My brother is bigger than yours.

The adjectives **anden**, other, different; **anderledes**, different; and **forskellig**,
different, dissimilar, also express dissimilarity:

De to søskende er meget forskellige.   The two siblings are very different.

3 Reinforcement:

stadig + comparative	**Kvaliteten blev stadig værre.**
ever	The quality got ever worse.
aller- + superlative	**Han var min allerbedste ven.**
very	He was my very best friend.

62   INFLEXION OF THE SUPERLATIVE

In the same way as other adjectives in the positive form, the superlative
inflects in the definite, adding an **-e**:

Det er den kedeligste bog jeg har læst.
That is the most boring book I have read.

Det var en af de mest fantastiske forestillinger jeg nogensinde har set.
That was one of the most fantastic performances I've ever seen.

Note: The adjectives **bedste, første, sidste** are often used without a front article, see
53, Type 3.

63   THE ABSOLUTE COMPARATIVE AND ABSOLUTE SUPERLATIVE

When the second part of the comparative or superlative is not stated, the element of comparison may disappear. The comparative then often equates to English phrases with 'rather', 'fairly', etc.:

Min onkel er en ældre mand.	My uncle is an elderly man.
Han lånte en større sum penge.	He borrowed a rather large sum of money.

Others: **en bedre middag**, a rather good dinner; **en længere samtale**, quite a long conversation.

The superlative often equates to English phrases with 'very', etc.:

med det venligste smil	with a very friendly smile
med største fornøjelse	with very great pleasure
Jan og Marie er de bedste venner.	Jan and Marie are the best of friends.

4 NUMERALS

64 CARDINAL AND ORDINAL NUMBERS

1 Cardinal and ordinal numbers:

	Cardinal numbers	*Ordinal numbers*
0	**nul**	
1	**en/et**	**første**
2	**to**	**anden, andet**
3	**tre**	**tredje**
4	**fire**	**fjerde**
5	**fem**	**femte**
6	**seks**	**sjette**
7	**syv**	**syvende**
8	**otte**	**ottende**
9	**ni**	**niende**
10	**ti**	**tiende**
11	**el(le)ve** ['elvə]	**el(le)vte**
12	**tolv** [tɔl']	**tolvte**
13	**tretten**	**trettende**
14	**fjorten**	**fjortende**
15	**femten**	**femtende**
16	**seksten** ['saisdən]	**sekstende**
17	**sytten**	**syttende**
18	**atten**	**attende**
19	**nitten**	**nittende**
20	**tyve**	**tyvende**
21	**enogtyve**	**enogtyvende**
22	**toogtyve**	**toogtyvende**
30	**tred(i)ve**	**tred(i)vte**
40	**fyrre**	**fyrretyvende**
50	**halvtreds** [hal'tres]	**halvtredsindstyvende**
60	**tres**	**tresindstyvende**
70	**halvfjerds**	**halvfjerdsindstyvende**
80	**firs**	**firsindstyvende**
90	**halvfems**	**halvfemsindstyvende**
100	**(et) hundrede**	**hundrede**
101	**(et) hundred(e) og en/et**	
125	**(et) hundred(e) og femogtyve**	

200	**to hundrede**	
1 000	**(et) tusind(e)**	**tusinde**
1 000 000	**en million**	**millionte**
1 000 000 000	**en milliard**	**milliardende**

2 The units come before the tens in Danish, and numerals under 100 are written as one word.

seksogtyve   twenty-six

3 The gap (or full stop) between the thousands in numbers written as figures corresponds to the English comma:

6 000 000 (6.000.000)   6,000,000

4 The numerals from 50 to 100 often cause confusion. They are based on a system of scores (20s):

halvtredsindstyve, usually abbreviated **halvtreds**, means '2½ times 20', i.e. 50.

tresindstyve, usually abbreviated **tres**, means '3 times 20', i.e. 60.

halvfjerdsindstyve, usually abbreviated **halvfjerds**, means '3½ times 20', i.e. 70.

firsindstyve, usually abbreviated **firs**, means '4 times 20', i.e. 80.

halvfemsindstyve, usually abbreviated **halvfems**, means '4½ times 20', i.e. 90.

In this system large numbers such as telephone numbers may at times prove opaque to learners: **94 57 71 82** = **fireoghalvfems, syvoghalvtreds, enoghalvfjerds, toogfirs**.

5 A simpler system for writing numerals is used by Danes in commerce and inter-Nordic contexts:

20 **toti**, 30 **treti**, 40 **firti**, 50 **femti**, 60 **seksti**, 70 **syvti**, 80 **otti**, 90 **niti** 25 **totifem**, etc.

6 The numeral **én** 'one' is often given an accent to distinguish it from the indefinite article **en** a(n), and inflects according to the gender of the following noun: **ét år**, one year; **hundredeogét år**, 101 years. Agreement of **én** does not occur in other compound numerals: **énogtyve børn**, 21 children.

7 The ordinal numbers **et hundrede, et tusind(e)** usually have plurals in **-r** when used in the sense 'hundreds/thousands of'.

The ordinal numbers **en million, en milliard** have plurals in **-er**.

65   MAJOR USES OF CARDINAL AND ORDINAL NUMBERS

1 Telephone numbers (see also **64.4**):
These are given in pairs:

52 19 77   **tooghalvtreds – nitten – syvoghalvfjerds**

2 Dates:

mandag den/d. 5. april
or: **mandag den 5.4**
or: **den femte i fjerde**
or: **5/4**
1993   **nittenhundrede og treoghalvfems** or: **nittentreoghalvfems**

3 Temperature:

Det fryser 10 grader.
Det er 10 graders frost/kulde.   } It's 10 degrees below zero.
Det er minus 10 grader.
Det er 30 graders varme.
Det er 30 grader varmt.   } It's 30 degrees.

But:

Han har 40 graders feber.   He has a temperature of 40 degrees.
Han har 40 i feber.

4 Money:

1,25 kr   **en krone og femogtyve** or: **én femogtyve**
25 kr   **femogtyve kroner**
1,50 kr   **halvanden krone**
2,50 kr   **to en halv (krone)**
6,75 kr   **seks (kroner og) femoghalvfjerds**
25,95 kr   **femogtyve (kroner og) femoghalvfems**
165,55 kr   **(et) hundrede og femogtres (kroner og) femoghalvtreds**

en hundredkroneseddel, a 100-kroner note
en tier, a 10-kroner coin
en femmer, a 5-kroner coin

Note: The nouns ending in **-er** (pl. **-e**) are used to indicate number generally:

Vi tager en toer til arbejdet.   We take a number two (bus) to work.

5 Fractions, decimals:
These are formed from ordinal numbers by adding **-del(e)**:

½   **en halv, halvdelen**
¼   **en fjerdedel/kvart**
⅗   **tre femtedele**
⅛   **en ottendedel**

halv inflects: **en halv pære** half a pear; **et halvt æble** half an apple; **den halve tid** half the time.

Notice: 1½ = **halvanden** or: **én og en halv**.

A comma is used where English has a decimal point:

0,45   **nul komma fire fem/nul komma femogfyrre**

6 Decades, centuries:

in the 1800s (nineteenth century)	**i det nittende (19.) århundrede (i 1800-tallet)**
in the 1900s (twentieth century)	**i det tyvende (20.) århundrede (i 1900-tallet)**
in the 1880s	**i 1880'erne (i attenhundrede og firserne)**
in the 90s	**i 90'erne (i halvfemserne)**
a woman in her fifties	**en kvinde i halvtredserne**

7 Others:

et syvtal, a figure 7	**en halv snes**, 10
et par, a pair	**en snes**, 20
et dusin, a dozen	**en gang, to gange**, once, twice

66   TIME BY THE CLOCK

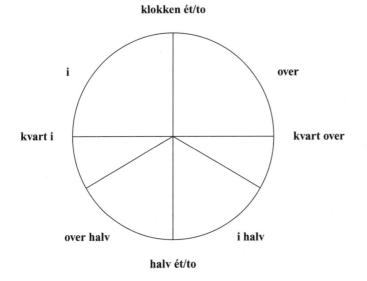

klokken ét/to

i

over

kvart i

kvart over

over halv

i halv

halv ét/to

Hvad er klokken?	What's the time?
Den/Klokken er (præcis) ti.	It's (exactly) ten o'clock.

Den/Klokken er ti minutter over tre.	It's ten past three.
Den/Klokken er syv minutter i fem.	It's seven minutes to five.
Den/Klokken er et kvarter i/over tolv.	It's a quarter to/past twelve.
Den/Klokken er halv syv.	It's half past six.
Den/Klokken er fem minutter i halv syv.	It's twenty-five past six.
Den/Klokken er fem minutter over halv syv.	It's twenty-five to seven.
Den/Klokken er mange.	It's late.
Hvad/Hvilken tid kører toget?	What time does the train leave?
13.00 (tretten nul nul)	thirteen hundred hours, i.e. 1 pm

5 PRONOUNS

67 PERSONAL AND REFLEXIVE PRONOUNS – FORM

Subject pronouns		*Object pronouns*		*Reflexive pronouns*	
Singular					
1 **jeg**	I	**mig**	me	**mig**	me, myself
2 **du**	you	**dig**	you	**dig**	you(rself)
De	you	**Dem**	you	**Dem**	you(rself)
3 **han**	he	**ham**	him	**sig**	him(self)
hun	she	**hende**	her	**sig**	her(self)
den	it	**den**	it	**sig**	it(self)
det	it	**det**	it	**sig**	it(self)
Plural					
1 **vi**	we	**os**	us	**os**	us, ourselves
2 **I**	you	**jer**	you	**jer**	you(rselves)
De	you	**Dem**	you	**Dem**	you(rselves)
3 **de**	they	**dem**	them	**sig**	them(selves)

Notes:

1 Pronunciation:

jeg [jai]	**De, de** [di]	**det** [de]
mig [mai]	**dig** [dai]	**sig** [sai]

2 Unlike English 'I', **jeg** does not have a capital letter except at the beginning of a sentence.

3 **De** and **Dem**, the polite forms, always have capital initial letters, as does **I**.

4 **I** is the plural of **du**, the familiar form.

68 USE OF PERSONAL PRONOUNS

1 **du/De**: these are used to address people. Most people now use the familiar **du**, notably at school, work, in the family and among friends. **De** is used to strangers, in formal situations such as official communications, to elderly people, and when surnames are used to address people (e.g. **Undskyld,**

hr./fru Hansen, har De set min kat?, Excuse me, Mr/Mrs Hansen, have you seen my cat?). Note also the following idiomatic expressions:

Du, kan du lige holde mit glas?
Hey you, could you just hold my glass?

Kære du, vil du ikke hjælpe mig?
My dear, will you please help me?

The polite form **De** is both singular and plural.

2 **han/hun**: these are not used to refer to so-called 'higher animals' or countries, unlike English. Notice that countries are neuter (to agree with **et land**): **Danmark er dyrt, men dejligt** Denmark is expensive, but lovely.

3 **den/det/de**: in addition to serving as personal pronouns, these words are also used as front articles (see **38**) and as demonstrative pronouns (see **74**), but **den** is never used to refer to a person. When referring to neuter nouns denoting people such as **et barn** or **et menneske**, **han** or **hun** is used.
Examples of usage:

Knud har købt *en ny bil.*	***Den* er meget stor.**
Knud has bought a new car.	It's very big.
Knud har købt *et nyt hus.*	***Det* er meget stort.**
Knud has bought a new house.	It's very big.
Knud har *to hunde.*	***De* er meget store.**
Knud has two dogs.	They are very big.
Knud har *et barn.*	***Hun* hedder Sonja.**
Knud has a child.	She is called Sonja.

4 The object form is used as subject complement in the following cases:

Hvem er det? Det er *mig.*	Who is it. It's me.
Det er *ham* der er den ældste.	It is he who is the eldest.

69   USES OF **DET**

In addition to serving as a pronoun referring back to a previously mentioned noun, **det** has a number of idiomatic usages:

1 As the subject of **være/blive** when the verb is followed by a noun, a pronoun or an adjective, irrespective of gender or number:

Hvem er hun? *Det* er min mor.	Who's she? It's my mother.
Hvad blev det? *Det* blev en pige.	What was it? It was a girl (*of a birth*).
Hvem er størst? *Det* er Viggo.	Who is the tallest? Viggo is.

2 As the formal subject of an infinitive (phrase):

Det er svært at lære dansk.   It's hard to learn Danish.

Note, however, that **der** is also used as a formal subject in certain cases, notably with the passive and with indefinite real subjects (see **142**):

Der drikkes meget øl i Danmark.   A lot of beer is drunk in Denmark.
Der hænger et billede på væggen.   A painting is hanging on the wall.

Danish uses **der** + an intransitive verb in this way while English generally uses only 'there' + the verb 'to be':

Der bor mange indvandrere her.   There are a lot of immigrants here.

3 As an impersonal subject:

Det blæser/hagler/regner/sner.   It is windy/hailing/raining/snowing.
Det ringer/banker på døren.   There's a ring on the door bell/
                                 a knock at the door.

Det ser ud til at han er syg.   It looks as if he's ill.
Hvordan går det? Det går fint.   How are you?/How are things?
                                 Fine.

4 As an object of verbs meaning 'believe', 'fear', 'hope', 'say', 'think', etc. (cf. English 'so'):

Fik han jobbet?   **Det frygter/håber/siger/tror de.**
Did he get the job?   They fear/hope/say/believe so.

Note also:

Per er dansker, og *det* er Pia også.   Per is a Dane and so is Pia.

5 In answer to questions, without an English equivalent, as a complement of **være/blive** or as an object of other auxiliary verbs:

Er du træt? Nej, *det* er jeg ikke.   Are you tired? No, I'm not.
Kan du tale dansk? Ja, *det* kan jeg. Do you speak Danish? Yes, I do.
Kommer de i aften? Ja, *det* gør de.   Are they coming tonight? Yes, they
                                         are.

Note also:

Hun ser venlig ud, og *det* er hun også.
She looks kind, and so she is.

6 When referring back to a whole clause:

Han hævder at han bor i Amerika, men *det* gør han ikke.
He claims that he lives in America, but he doesn't.

70   REFLEXIVE PRONOUNS

See also reflexive verbs, **103.5**.

The reflexive pronoun is used as direct/indirect object or prepositional complement when it is identical in meaning to the subject. Reflexive forms are identical to object forms in the first and second person, but in the third person (singular and plural) **sig** is used.

Jeg faldt og slog mig.	I fell and hurt myself
Du skal lukke døren efter dig!	You must close the door behind you!
Hun har lige vasket sig.	She has just washed (herself).
Vi morede os meget i aftes.	We enjoyed ourselves a lot last night.
Skynd jer!	Hurry up!
De havde ingen penge på sig.	They had no money on them.

It is important that the reflexive forms are used correctly. There is a lot of difference in meaning between **Han skød ham**, He shot him (i.e. someone else) and **Han skød sig**, He shot himself.

There is one notable exception to the main rule. After a verb followed by an object + infinitive construction, a reflexive pronoun refers to the object of the main verb (i.e. the subject of the infinitive – here: **Peter**), but a personal pronoun to the subject of the main clause (here: **Jens**):

Jens (S) **bad Peter** (O) **vaske sig.** (reflexive pronoun)
Jens asked Peter to wash (himself). (i.e. Peter to be washed)

Jens (S) **bad Peter** (O) **vaske ham.** (personal pronoun)
Jens asked Peter to wash him. (i.e. Jens to be washed)

The reflexive pronouns are used with a number of verbs in Danish (see **103.5**) where the reflexive idea is absent in English: **barbere sig**, shave; **gifte sig**, get married; **glæde sig**, look forward; **kede sig**, be bored; **lægge/ sætte sig**, lie/sit down; **opføre sig**, behave; **rejse sig**, get/stand up; **ærgre sig**, be/feel annoyed; **øve sig**, practise, etc.

Reflexive pronouns are always unstressed. If emphasis is needed, for example, to indicate a contrast or lack of assistance, the word **selv** is added to the reflexive pronoun. Note that English often uses 'own':

Kan han vaske sig selv?	Can he wash himself?
Hun redte sig selv.	She combed her own hair.
De lærte at sminke sig selv.	They learnt to do their own make-up.

Selv can also function more independently, referring to nouns or pronouns. Like **sig**, it is gender-neutral and it is always stressed:

Per skrev artiklen selv.	Per wrote the article himself.
Du kan selv vælge menuen.	You can choose the menu yourself.
Selv har jeg aldrig set ham.	I myself have never seen him.
Det var hende selv der sagde det.	It was she herself who said it.

71 RECIPROCAL PRONOUNS

Modern Danish has in effect only one reciprocal pronoun: **hinanden** 'each other'. Unlike the reflexive pronouns, which are used in connection with a simple action/state, **hinanden** implies a mutual action/state between two or more individuals or things. **Hinanden** refers back to a plural subject and can never itself be the subject of the clause. It has a genitive form: **hinandens**.

De elsker hinanden.	They love each other.
Vi gav hinanden hånden.	We shook hands.
Stoler I på hinanden?	Do you trust each other?
De har mødt hinandens børn.	They have met each other's children.

Until recently, **hverandre** was used to refer to more than two. It is now very formal and old-fashioned.

72 POSSESSIVE PRONOUNS

Possessive pronouns have the same form irrespective of position. Unlike English, there is thus no formal distinction between attributive and predicative use:

Det er min bog.	It is my book.
Bogen er min.	The book is mine.

First and second person possessives agree in form with the noun:

Det er *din* **bil,** *dit* **hus og** *dine* **penge.**
Cf. *en* **bil,** *et* **hus, penge** (pl.)
It is your car, your house and your money.

Third person possessives ending in **-s** do not inflect:

Det er hans/hendes bil, hans/hendes hus og hans/hendes penge.
It is his/her car, his/her house and his/her money.

The reflexive forms **sin**, **sit**, **sine** are explained more fully in **73**.

		Common gender	Neuter	Plural	
Singular					
1		**min**	**mit**	**mine**	my, mine
2	familiar	**din**	**dit**	**dine**	your, yours
	formal	**Deres**	**Deres**	**Deres**	your, yours
3	masculine	**hans/sin**	**hans/sit**	**hans/sine**	his
	feminine	**hendes/sin**	**hendes/sit**	**hendes/sine**	her, hers
	non-human	**dens/sin**	**dets/sit**	**dens/dets/sine**	its

	Common gender	Neuter	Plural	
Plural				
1	**vores** (**vor**)	**vores** (**vort**)	**vores** (**vore**)	our, ours
2 familiar	**jeres** (**jer**)	**jeres** (**jert**)	**jeres** (**jere**)	your, yours
formal	**Deres**	**Deres**	**Deres**	your, yours
3	**deres**	**deres**	**deres**	their, theirs

Notes:

1 Possessive pronouns have genitive meaning and therefore no separate genitive form:

dine forældres bøger   your parents' books
dine bøger   your books

2 The second person forms **din**, **dit**, **dine** correspond to **du**; **jeres** corresponds to **I**; **Deres** corresponds to **De**; but **jer**, **jert**, **jere** are now obsolete.

3 The third person form **deres** corresponds to **de**.

4 The form **vores** is found in modern everyday Danish; **vor**, **vort**, **vore** tend to be found in formal Danish and fixed expressions:

Vores børn er voksne nu.   Our children are adults now.
Vores have er dejlig om sommeren. Our garden is lovely in summer.

But often:

vor dronning, **vort modersmål**, **vore**   our Queen/mother tongue/ancestors
    forfædre

Note also: **i vor tid/i vore dage**, in our time, nowadays; **Vor Herre/Vorherre**, Our Lord.

5 **dens**, **dets** are used of animals and inanimate objects:

Hunden er såret. *Dens* **ben bløder.**   The dog is injured. Its leg is bleeding.
Huset er gammelt, men *dets* **tag er nyt.**   The house is old but its roof is new.

6 English possessive pronouns modifying words for parts of the body or articles of clothing are usually rendered by the definite article in Danish if there is no doubt about the ownership:

Han har brækket armen.   He has broken his arm.
Tag skoene af!   Take off your shoes!

73   NON-REFLEXIVE AND REFLEXIVE POSSESSIVES: **HANS** OR **SIN**?

1 The reflexive forms **sin/sit/sine** modify an object or a prepositional complement and refer to the subject of the clause with which it is identical in meaning:

Han elsker *sin* kone, *sit* barn og *sine* forældre.

S ←————|————|.————|

He loves his wife, his child and his parents.

Notice that **sin/sit/sine** cannot be used to refer to a plural subject:

De elsker deres mor.	They love their mother.
De har glemt deres penge.	They have forgotten their money.

Sin/sit/sine cannot be used to modify the subject of the clause, i.e. it cannot be part of it; **hans** (etc.) is used instead:

Hans datter hentede ham.   His daughter fetched him.
　　S

2 The non-reflexive forms do not refer back to the subject of the clause they appear in; here **sin/sit/sine** must be used.
　Compare:

Reflexive:
Svend tog på ferie med *sin* kone.
　S
Svend went on holiday with his (own) wife.

Non-reflexive:
Ole er sur, fordi Svend tog på ferie med *hans* kone.
　S　　　　/SC　　S
Ole is in a bad mood because Svend went on holiday with his
　(i.e. Ole's) wife.

The non-reflexive, third person possessive pronouns **hans, hendes, dens/dets, deres** may modify the subject (S), the subject complement (SComp.), the object (O) or a prepositional complement (Prep.Comp.):

Hans kone er lærer. 　　S	His wife is a teacher.
Bageren var *hendes* søn. 　　　　(SComp.)	The baker was her son.
Jeg mødte *hendes* mand i byen. 　　　　　O	I met her husband in town.
De er glade for *deres* børn. 　　　　(Prep.Comp.)	They are fond of their children.

There are two simple ways of testing which form to use in the third person singular:

(a) Draw an arrow to the referent of the pronoun (which the pronoun must not modify). Is the referent the subject of that clause? If so, use a form of **sin/sit/sine**; if not, then use a non-reflexive form.

(b) Can you insert the word 'own' before the modified noun in English? If so, use a form of **sin/sit/sine**; if not, then use a non-reflexive form.

3 A problem arises when there is more than one clause in the sentence:

> She thinks that *her* son is lovely.   **Hun synes at *hendes* søn er dejlig.**
> S   /SC   S

Here 'her' is not in the same clause as 'she' (the subject of the main clause), but modifies 'son' as part of the subject of the subordinate clause ('her son'). Therefore use **hendes**.

> Cf. **Hun elsker *sin* søn.**   She loves her son.
>   S   O

4 The main rule also applies when the possessive precedes the subject:

> **Til *sin* fødselsdag fik *hun* et ur.**   For her birthday she got a watch.
>   ──────────────────→ S

5 In object + infinitive constructions, **sin/sit/sine** may refer to the subject of the infinitive (InfS):

> Lone heard her call her husband.   **Lone hørte *hende* kalde på *sin* mand.**
>   (i.e. not Lone's husband) S   InfS ←───── Prep.Comp.

> John saw him kick his dog.   **John så *ham* sparke *sin* hund.**
>   (i.e. not John's dog) S   InfS ←───── O

To test this, expand the ellipted clause into a full clause and apply the main rule:

> **Jeg så at han sparkede *sin* hund.**
> S   /SC S ←──────── O

6 **Sin/sit/sine** may also have general reference:

> **Det er ikke let at elske *sin* næste.**   Loving your neighbour is not easy.
> **At betale *sine* regninger er vigtigt.**   To pay one's bills is important.

7 Note the use of **sin/sit/sine** in abbreviated comparisons:

> **Han er højere end *sin* kone.**   He is taller than his wife.
> Cf. **Han er højere end hans kone er.**   He is taller than his wife is.

8 Note the use of **sin/sit/sine** in expressions with **hver sin**, etc. However, here the appropriate plural pronoun is increasingly used, i.e. **hver vores/jeres/deres**:

> **Vi fik hver *sine/vores* møbler.**   We each got our own furniture.
> **I kan vælge hver *sin/jeres* menu.**   You may each choose your own
>   menu.

Pigerne sov i hver *sit/deres* **værelse.**   Each of the girls slept in her/their
own room.

Notice that **hver** is indeclinable in such phrases, and that the choice of
sin/sit/sine is determined by the gender/number of the noun modified.

74   DEMONSTRATIVE PRONOUNS

	Common gender	Neuter	Plural
'Near'	**denne (her), den her**	**dette (her), det her**	**disse (her), de her**
	this	this	these
'Distant'	**den (der)**	**det (der)**	**de (der)**
	that	that	those

1 The main difference between the two sets of demonstratives (**denne/
dette/disse** vs. **den/det/de**) is one of proximity or distance (in space or
time) from the speaker. This may be emphasised by the addition of **her**
(nearby) or **der** (further away). Demonstratives are always stressed and
often have an identifying or 'pointing' function.

Denne vase er meget gammel.   This vase is very old.
Den (der) på bordet er ganske ny.   The one on the table is quite new.

2 The addition of **her/der** makes the demonstrative much more colloquial,
especially when preceding a noun. They are therefore mostly used when
the noun is omitted.

Jeg mener *denne* **bog, ikke** *den der.*   I mean this book, not that one.

3 As in English, the demonstratives may be used attributively or predicatively (i.e. independently of a noun). They then take the number/gender
of the noun to which they refer:

Hvad koster *de* **bananer?**   What do those bananas cost?
Er de billigere end *de her?*   Are they cheaper than these?
Dette **er noget nyt.**   This is something new.
Jeg tager *dette* **kort, ikke** *det der.*   I'll take this card, not that one.

4 The demonstrative is often used in Danish to direct attention to a
following restrictive (i.e. necessary) relative clause. In these cases it
replaces the usual end article, but younger Danes increasingly use the end
article in these cases:

Den **elev som fik de højeste karakterer, er min nabo.**
   (Or: **Eleven ...**)
The pupil who got the highest marks is my neighbour.

Det **bælte hun købte i går, passer ikke til hendes nye kjole.**
(Or: **Bæltet ...**)
The belt she bought yesterday does go with her new dress.

If the relative clause is non-restrictive (i.e. not strictly necessary), only an end article is possible:

Træerne, som i øvrigt snart skal fældes, skygger for udsigten.
The trees, which incidentally will be cut down soon, are blocking the
view.

5 The demonstrative is also used to refer to a following **at-** clause:

Vi traf *den* beslutning at firmaet måtte lukke.
We took the decision that the firm had to close down.

6 When referring to people, the genitive forms **dennes, disses** may be found in formal Danish:

Dennes/Disses **udtalelser var interessante.**
This person's/These people's statements were interesting.

7 **Dennes (ds.)** also means 'inst.' (this month):

Jvf. vores brev af den 10. *dennes* **(ds.).**
Cf. our letter of the 10th inst.

8 **Den** is used independently of a person in proverbs, etc.:

Den **der ler sidst, ler bedst.**   He who laughs last laughs longest.

9 Note that the object form of **de** (when not followed by a noun) is **dem**:

De sko? Nej, *dem* **har jeg aldrig set før!**
Those shoes! No, I've never seen those before!

10 Note also the following idiomatic phrases:

den og den person/dato (etc.)   such and such a person/date (etc.)
på det og det tidspunkt   at such and such a time

75 RELATIVE PRONOUNS

Relative pronouns introduce a subordinate relative clause and usually refer back to a correlative (corr.) in the main clause:

Jeg har en ven /som er læge.   I have a friend who is a doctor.
              corr.

Relative pronouns include:

der	who, which, that
som	who(m), which, that
hvis	whose
hvem	who(m)
hvad	what, which
hvilken/hvilket/hvilke	(who(m)), which

Note that **hvor** (where) is a relative adverb.

There are two types of relative clause: restrictive and non-restrictive. A restrictive relative clause is necessary in order to identify the correlative and therefore cannot be omitted. In a non-restrictive (or parenthetical) relative clause the correlative is known, so the relative clause merely provides extra information and can be omitted. Compare:

Restrictive:
Min kollega *som* bor på Amager, tager bussen til arbejde.
My colleague who lives on (the island of) Amager takes the bus to work. (one of several)

Non-restrictive:
Min mor, *som* nu er meget gammel, bor på plejehjem.
My mother, who is now very old, lives in a nursing home. (identity not in doubt)

According to the rules of the 'new comma' (see **171**) there is no comma before a restrictive clause.

Examples of use:

1 **Kan du se den dreng *der* leger derhenne?** (Or: **drengen ...**)
  Can you see the boy who is playing over there?

2 **Det hus *som* ligger på hjørnet, har røde mursten.** (Or: **Huset ...**)
  The house that stands on the corner has red bricks.

3 **Den film (*som*) vi så i går, var meget morsom.** (Or: **Filmen ...**)
  The film (that) we saw yesterday was very funny.

4 **Vores børn, *som* I vist ikke har set, går i skole nu.**
  Our children, who(m) you haven't seen, I suppose, now go to school.

5 **Den vej (*som*) hun bor på, går forbi kirken.** (Or: **Vejen ...**)
  The road (that) she lives in goes past the church.

6 **Kirsten, *hvis* datter skal giftes, er alvorligt syg.**
  Kirsten, whose daughter is getting married, is seriously ill.

7 **Hanne kommer fra den by *hvis* navn jeg ikke kan udtale.**
  Hanne comes from the town whose name I can't pronounce.

8 **Hun er den kvinde med *hvem* jeg helst vil rejse til Rom.**
She is the woman with whom I most want to go to Rome.

9 **Han spiser med fingrene, *hvad* der ikke ser pænt ud.**
He eats with his fingers, which doesn't look very nice.

10 **Han ønsker selv reparere taget, *hvad* han ikke kan.**
He wants to repair the roof himself, which he can't do.

11 **Gør *hvad* du vil!**
Do what you want!

12 **Det er det hus i *hvilket* Per boede.**
That is the house in which Per lived.

13 **Helle siger at Palle ikke kan svømme, *hvilket* er noget sludder.**
Helle says that Palle can't swim, which is nonsense.

Notes:

1 **der** is only used as subject (example 1). See **76**.

2 **som** may be omitted from a restrictive relative clause when it is not the subject (examples 3, 5). See **76**.

3 A preposition cannot appear in the same clause directly before **som**, but may be placed at the end of the clause, whether **som** is omitted or not (example 5). See **76**.

4 A preposition may precede **hvem** and **hvilken** in formal Danish (examples 8, 12).

5 **hvis** is found mainly in written Danish and refers to both animate and inanimate nouns (examples 6, 7).

6 **hvem** can only refer to humans (example 8); **hvad** and (largely) **hvilken** refer to non-humans (examples 9–13).

7 In a non-restrictive clause, **hvad** and **hvilken** can refer back to the whole of the previous clause (examples 9, 10, 13).

8 When **hvad** is the subject of the relative clause, it must be followed by **der** (example 9).

9 **hvad** can also refer to some following information (cataphoric reference):

   Men *hvad* han ikke fortalte os var at han skal opereres.
   But what he didn't tell us was that he is going to have an operation.

10 Note the frequent construction: **alt hvad** (all that):

   Hun gjorde alt hvad hun kunne.   She did all that she could.

11 **hvilken** is the only relative pronoun that inflects for gender/number. It is only used in formal written language: **hvilken** (common gender, sing.); **hvilket** (neuter, sing.); **hvilke** (plural).

12 Note that **hvem, hvad, hvilken, hvis** are also interrogative pronouns. See **77**.

76 DER OR SOM?

Both words have uses other than that of a relative pronoun: **der** can function as a formal subject (**Der sidder en fugl på min cykel**, There's a bird sitting on my bike), and as an adverb of place (**Hun står lige der**, She is standing just there); while **som** may be a conjunction (**Svend er lige så stor som sin søster**, Svend is just as tall as his sister). See **107, 134, 142**.

Der can only be the subject in a relative clause. In this function either **der** or **som** may be used, though **der** is more common in spoken Danish. They can introduce both restrictive and non-restrictive clauses:

Restrictive:
Så du den kamp *der/som* blev vist i fjernsynet i aftes?
Did you watch the match that was shown on TV last night?

Non-restrictive:
Min bedste ven, *der/som* lige har fået et nyt job, har købt hus.
My best friend, who has just got a new job, has bought a house.

However, when there are two coordinated relative clauses, **der** cannot be used in the second one:

Det er en vin *der/som* kan drikkes nu, men *som* også kan gemmes.
This is a wine that can be drunk now, but which may also be laid down.

Som can function as subject, direct/indirect object or prepositional complement in the relative clause. When it is a prepositional complement, the preposition cannot precede **som**, but must come after the verb. **Som** cannot be omitted when it introduces a non-restrictive clause.

Jeg har en veninde, *som* er utrolig sød. (subject)
I have a girlfriend who is incredibly nice.

Jeg har en veninde, *som* jeg besøger hver måned. (direct object)
I have a girlfriend whom I visit every month.

Jeg har en veninde, *som* jeg giver mange gaver. (indirect object)
I have a girlfriend whom I give many presents to.

Jeg har en veninde, *som* jeg ofte skriver til. (Prep.Comp.)
I have a girlfriend whom I often write to.

In a restricted clause, when it is not the subject, **som** may (optionally) be left out:

Den bog (*som*) jeg købte i fredags, er blevet væk. (direct object)
The book (that) I bought on Friday has gone missing.

Har du set de bure (*som*) de holder løver i? (Prep.Comp.)
Have you seen the cages (which) they keep lions in?

77 INTERROGATIVE PRONOUNS (**HV-** WORDS)

Interrogative pronouns introduce a direct or indirect question.
Interrogative pronouns (**hv-** words) include:

Common gender	Neuter	Plural	Genitive
hvem	**hvad**	**hvem**	**hvis**
who(m)	what	who(m)	whose
hvilken	**hvilket**	**hvilke**	
what/which	what/which	what/which	
hvad for en	**hvad for et**	**hvad for nogle**	
which (kind/one)	which (kind/one)	which (kinds/ones)	

Note that **hvor**, where; **hvordan**, how; **hvorfor**, why; and **hvornår**, when;
are interrogative adverbs.
Examples of use:

Hvem er det?	Who is it?
Hvem talte du med?	Who(m) did you talk to?
Hun spurgte hvem der ringede.	She asked who phoned.
Hvad er klokken?	What's the time?
Kan du se hvad Dorte laver?	Can you see what Dorte is doing?
Hvad for en bog vil De have?	What kind of/Which book do you want?
Hvad for nogle børn har de?	What kind of children do they have?
Hvilken skole går Deres søn i?	Which school does your son go to?
Hvis hat er det?	Whose hat is it?
De vidste ikke hvis (hat) det var.	They didn't know whose (hat) it was.

Notes:

1 **hvilken** (etc.) is mostly found in written Danish; **hvad for en** (etc.) in colloquial language.

2 **hvem** and **hvad** must add **der**, when they are the subject in a subordinate clause (indirect question):

Jeg hørte ikke hvem der vandt.	I didn't hear who won.
Han spurgte hvad der var sket.	He asked what had happened.

3 For emphasis, **hvem, hvad, hvilken** may add **som helst**:

Hvem som helst kan komme til festen.	Anyone may come to the party.

78   INDEFINITE PRONOUNS

Indefinite pronouns include the following:

Common gender	Neuter	Plural	
al	alt, alting	alle	all, everything, everyone
		begge	both
(en)hver	hvert		each, every(one)
ingen	intet,	ingen	no, none, no one,
	ingenting		nothing
	lidt	få	little, few
man			one, you, they
megen, meget	meget	mange	much, very, many
nogen	noget	nogle (nogen)	some/any, something/
			anything, someone/
			anyone

1 Al, alt, alle

(a) **Al** is only used with non-count nouns: **al den snak/støj**, all that talk/noise.

(b) **Alt** 'all', 'everything' is very common, while **alting** is used for emphasis:

Fortæl mig *alt*!	Tell me everything!
Hvor er *alt* **mit tøj?**	Where are all my clothes?
Alting **er forbi!**	Everything is at an end!

Note also: **i alt**, in all; **alt i alt**, all in all; **alt for**, too; **alt hvad**, all that; **alt vel**, everything OK; **frem for alt**, above all; **trods alt**, despite everything.

(c) **Alle** 'all', 'everybody', 'everyone' can appear attributively, nominally and in the genitive:

Alle **børn går i skole.**	All children go to school.
Alle **kom til tiden.**	Everybody arrived on time.
Nu skal vi *alle* **hjem og spise.**	We are all going home to eat now.
Det er ikke *alles* **yndlingsmusik.**	It's not everyone's favourite music.

Note also: **alle og enhver**, all and sundry; **alle sammen**, one and all; **alle steder/vegne**, everywhere; **alle tiders**, fantastic, of all time; **en gang for alle,** once and for all.

2 Begge

Begge is used both attributively and nominally; in nominal use it is sometimes, but not always, followed by **to** (two). It also has a genitive form: **begges**.

Begge **forældre(ne) går på arbejde.**	Both parents go to work.
Hun kan lide *begge* **dele.**	She likes both.

Jeg så *begge* **forestillinger(ne).**	I saw both (the) performances.
De er *begge (to)* **meget venlige.**	They are both very kind.
Begge (to) **gav deres samtykke.**	Both gave their consent.
De er voksne *begge to.*	They are both adults.
Begges **formue gik tabt.**	The fortune of both was lost.

NB: 'both . . . and' corresponds to **både . . . og**.

Charlotte kan *både* **læse** *og* **skrive.**	Charlotte can both read and write.

3 Hver, hvert, enhver

Hver/hvert is used both attributively and nominally; **enhver** has greater emphasis:

hver time/dag/uge/måned, every hour/day/week/month; **hvert minut/år**, every minute/year; **hver anden gang**, every second time; **hver især**, each one

Hver **(person) fik en gave.**	Each (person) got a present.
De fik en gave *hver.*	They got a present each.
De fik *hver* **en gave.**	They each got a present.
Det kan *enhver* **forstå.**	Anyone can understand that.
Der er noget for *enhver* **(smag).**	There is something for every(one's)/ taste.
Hver **mand/***Enhver* **sin lyst.**	Everyone to his taste.

4   Ingen, intet, ingenting

(a) **Ingen** is used with common gender and plural nouns, **intet** with neuter nouns; both can have nominal function. **Ingen, intet** are often replaced by **ikke nogen/noget** in spoken Danish:

De har *ingen* **børn/penge.**	They have no children/money.
Intet **nyt er godt nyt.**	No news is good news.
Jeg mødte *ikke nogen* **(mennesker).**	I didn't meet anyone/any people.
Vi har *ikke noget* **at spise.**	We have nothing to eat.
Ingen **har set ham i dag.**	No one has seen him today.

(b) **Ingenting** is colloquial and more emphatic than **intet/ikke noget**. It is only used nominally:

Jeg hørte *ingenting.*	I heard nothing.
Der er *ingenting* **i vejen.**	There's nothing wrong.
Det gør *ingenting.*	It doesn't matter.

5 Lidt, få

(a) **Lidt** denotes a small quantity and may appear with either common gender or neuter non-count nouns, or before adjectives, but it can also be used nominally. It has positive connotations (= English 'some'); to make

it more negative it may be preceded by **kun** or **meget**. For comparison
see **59**.

Har du *lidt* mælk?	Have you got some milk?
Jeg blev *lidt* sur.	I became a little bad tempered.
Der er kun *lidt* tilbage i flasken.	There's only a little left in the bottle.
Hun spiser meget *lidt*.	She eats very little.
Vil du have *lidt* mere?	Do you want a little more?
Der er tre søm for *lidt*.	There are three nails too few.

Note also: **Bliv/Vent lidt!**, Stay/Wait a little!; **lidt efter lidt**, little by little;
om lidt, in a moment.

(b) **Få** denotes a small number and is used with plural nouns or nominally.
It has negative connotations (= English '(very) few'), which may be empha-
sised by adding **kun** or **meget**. If **nogle** is added, it sounds more positive.
For comparison see **59**.

Der var *få* mennesker til stede.	There were few people present.
Der er kun *få* æbler på træet.	There are few apples on the tree.
Meget *få* mødte op.	Very few turned up.
Der er nogle *få* billetter tilbage.	There are a few tickets left.
Stykket er afgjort kun for de *få*.	The play is definitely only for the few.

6 Man

Man is third person singular and has general reference to humans (cf.
French 'on' and German 'man'). There is no single English equivalent,
but depending on the context 'you', 'one', 'we', 'they' or a passive construction may translate it. Outside the subject case, other forms are used:

Subject	*Object*	*Possessive*	*Reflexive*
man	**én**	**ens, sin/sit/sine**	**sig**

Man kører bare ligeud.	You just drive straight on.
Man ved aldrig hvad der kan ske.	You never know what might happen.
Man kan ikke vide alt.	One can't know everything.
I Italien spiser *man* meget pasta.	In Italy they eat a lot of pasta.
Man fangede tyven.	The thief was caught.
Kan *man* mon stole på det?	Is that reliable, I wonder?
Det giver *én* chancen for at vinde.	It gives one the chance to win.
***Éns* handlinger kan misforstås.**	One's actions may be misunderstood.
Man må gøre *sit* bedste.	One must do one's best.
Man kan vente *sig* meget af ham.	One can expect a lot from him.

As subject, **man** and **én** can be used in an affected and mock ironic way to replace **du/De** and **jeg**, respectively:

Man er nok i habit i dag!	So one is wearing a suit today!
Én føler sig lidt utilpas.	One feels a little unwell.

7 Megen, meget, mange

(a) **Megen** as the common gender form with non-count nouns is now increasingly being replaced by **meget**. It is still found in formal language:

Der var megen omtale af sagen.	There was much talk about the case.

(b) **Meget** is the general form in the singular, and is used to modify non-count nouns or adjectives, or it may have nominal function. For comparison see **59**:

Der er meget varmt i stuen.	It's very hot in the living room.
Det var en meget dårlig præstation.	It was a very bad performance.
Er der meget kaffe i kanden?	Is there a lot of coffee in the pot?
Der er meget at gøre.	There's much to do.
Hvor meget koster det?	How much is it?
Hvor meget er klokken?	What's the time?

Note that with some common adjectives (e.g. **god**, **pæn**, **sød**) **meget** can sometimes in spoken Danish act as a downtoner rather than an uptoner. If so, it receives stress and the adjective/adverb is part of a rising intonation:

Hvordan gik det? Det gik meget godt.
How did it go? It went all right. (but no more)

Er det ikke pænt? Jo, det er meget pænt.
Isn't it nice? Yes, it is quite nice. (but ...)

Before comparative forms, **meget** corresponds to 'much':

Deres have er meget større end min.
Their garden is much bigger than mine.

Note also: **Det er lige meget**, It doesn't matter; **mangt og meget**, a great many things.

(c) **Mange** is used with plural nouns to indicate an unspecified but substantial number. It can have attributive and nominal function. For comparison see **59**:

Der var mange mennesker i byen.	There were a lot of people in town.
Vi hørte mange gode forslag.	We heard a lot of good proposals.
Har hun mange penge?	Has she got a lot of money?

Kom der mange til foredraget?   Did many come to the talk?
Der er for mange fattige.   There are too many poor people.

Note also: **mange gange**, many times; **Klokken er mange**, It's late.

8 Nogen, noget, nogle

(a) **Nogen** has both attributive and nominal function. It may appear with common gender non-count nouns in the singular and with plural nouns when it has negative (or non-assertive) connotations (= English 'any(one)'). It therefore often appears with plural nouns in questions and after a negation. It has the genitive form **nogens**.

Det tog nogen tid at gøre det.	It took some time to do it.
Har du nogen cigaretter?	Have you got any cigarettes?
Der er ikke nogen hjemme.	There is no one at home.
Er der nogen der vil have mere kaffe?	Would anyone like more coffee?
Jeg kender ikke nogen der kan flyve.	I don't know anyone who can fly.
Er det nogens frakke?	Is that anyone's coat?

(b) **Noget** has also attributive and nominal function and may correspond to both 'something' and 'anything'. It can modify non-count nouns (including common gender ones) and adjectives:

Har du noget mad? (Cf. **maden**)	Have you got any food?
Der er sket noget alvorligt.	Something serious has happened.
Er der noget i vejen?	Is something/anything the matter?
Jeg har fået noget i øjet.	I've got something in my eye.

Note that **ikke nogen/noget** is often used for **ingen/intet** in spoken Danish, see **78.4**.

(c) **Nogle** (often pronounced like **nogen**) is, due to the conflation in pronunciation, largely restricted to the written language. Here it has positive (or assertive) connotations (= English 'some(one)'):

Her ligger nogle aviser.	There are some newspapers here.
Nogle mennesker bliver aldrig klogere.	Some people never get any wiser.
Nogle af børnene kom for sent.	Some of the children were late.
Der er nogle der snyder.	There are some (people) who cheat.
Efter nogles mening er det forkert.	In some people's view it's wrong.

Note that in attributive use **nogen** often has stress, whereas **nogle** is unstressed:

Har du 'nogen 'frimærker?	Have you got any stamps? (non-assertive)
Har du nogle 'frimærker?	Have you got some stamps? (assertive)

6 VERBS

VERBS FORMS

79 VERB FORMS IN OUTLINE

In modern Danish there is only one form for all persons, singular and plural, in each of the various tenses of the verb.

Danish has no continuous form of the verb (cf. **94**) and, like English, employs auxiliary verbs to help form the perfect, past perfect and future tenses (cf. **96ff**). For learning purposes it is a convenient simplification to consider the formation of the different verb forms as the addition of an ending to the basic part of the verb – the stem (see below).

There are four principal conjugations of Danish verbs. Conjugations I, II and III are weak conjugations, which form their past tense by means of an ending that adds another syllable to the word. Conjugation IV contains strong verbs, which form their past tense either without an ending (but often by changing the stem vowel) or by the ending **-t** which does not add an extra syllable. Below is a table summarising the endings for each conjugation and verb form (note that vowel stems have no infinitive **-e** ending):

Conjugation	Imperative = stem	Infinitive = stem + **e/zero**	Present tense = stem + **(e)r**	
Weak				
I	**lev!**	**leve**	**lever**	live, be alive
	tro!	**tro**	**tror**	believe, think
II	**spis!**	**spise**	**spiser**	eat
III	**læg!**	**lægge**	**lægger**	lay, put
Strong				
IV	**drik!**	**drikke**	**drikker**	drink
	løb!	**løbe**	**løber**	run
	skriv!	**skrive**	**skriver**	write
	vind!	**vinde**	**vinder**	win

Conjugation	Past tense	Past participle	Present participle
Weak	stem + **ede/te/de**	stem + **(e)t**	stem + **ende**
I	lev*ede*	lev*et*	lev*ende*
	tro*ede*	tro*et*	tro*ende*
II	spis*te*	spis*t*	spis*ende*
III	lag*de*	lag*t*	læg*gende*
Strong	stem (often with vowel change) + **zero/t**	stem (often with vowel change) + **et**	
IV	drak	drukk*et*	drikk*ende*
	løb	løb*et*	løb*ende*
	skrev	skrev*et*	skriv*ende*
	vand*t*	vund*et*	vind*ende*

80   FIRST CONJUGATION

Infinitive + **e/zero**	Present + **(e)r**	Past + **ede**	Past participle + **et**	Meaning
arbejde	**arbejder**	**arbejdede**	**arbejdet**	work
studere	**studerer**	**studerede**	**studeret**	study
tro	**tror**	**troede**	**troet**	believe, think

More than 80 per cent of weak verbs, and all new verbs, e.g. **jobbe**, work; **lifte**, hitchhike; belong to this conjugation, including those ending in **-ere**: **nationalisere**, nationalise; **parkere**, park.

Examples of frequent verbs in Conjugation I:

arbejde, work; **bygge**, build; **elske**, love; **forklare**, explain; **hade**, hate; **handle**, act, shop; **hente**, fetch; **huske**, remember; **lave**, do, make; **lege**, play; **lukke**, close; **pakke**, pack; **prøve**, try; **snakke**, chat, talk; **spille**, play; **vaske**, wash; **vente**, wait; **åbne**, open

Verbs ending in stressed **-e, -o, -æ, -ø, -å** in the infinitive add **-r** in the present:

sne – sner, snow; **bo – bor**, live, stay; **tø – tør**, thaw; **nå – når**, reach

Verbs ending in stressed **-i, -u, -y** in the infinitive add **-(e)r** in the present:

fri – fri(e)r, propose; **du – du(e)r**, be (any) good; **sy – sy(e)r**, sew

81   SECOND CONJUGATION

Infinitive + **e**	Present + **er**	Past + **te**	Past Participle + **t**	Meaning
kende	**kender**	**kendte**	**kendt**	know
køre	**kører**	**kørte**	**kørt**	drive
spise	**spiser**	**spiste**	**spist**	eat

About 10 per cent of Danish weak verbs belong to Conjugation II. They include:

1 Some verbs with stems ending in a long vowel (or a diphthong) + **-b**, soft **d**, soft **g**, **-l**, **-n**, **-r**, **-s**:

købe, buy; **råbe**, shout; **tabe**, lose; **bløde**, bleed; **brede**, spread; **føde**, give birth; **bruge**, use; **stege**, fry; **søge**, seek; **dele**, divide, share; **føle**, feel; **tale**, talk; **låne**, borrow, lend; **mene**, mean, think; **høre**, hear; **lære**, learn, teach; **læse**, read; **låse**, lock; **rejse**, go, travel; **vise**, show

2 Some verbs with a short vowel and a stem ending in **-l(d)**, **-m**, **-nd**, **-ng**:

bestille, do, order; **skille**, separate; **fylde**, fill; **kalde**, call; **glemme**, forget; **ramme**, hit; **begynde**, begin; **kende**, know; **hænge**, hang; **trænge**, need, push

3 A few verbs with a short vowel and a stem vowel in **-ls**, **-nk**:

frelse, save; **hilse**, greet; **tænke**, think

4 Very few verbs with a vowel stem:

ske, happen

5 A number of verbs with vowel change in the past tense:

Infinitive	Present	Past	Past Participle	Meaning
dølge	**dølger**	**dulgte**	**dulgt**	conceal
fortælle	**fortæller**	**fortalte**	**fortalt**	tell
følge	**følger**	**fulgte**	**fulgt**	follow
række	**rækker**	**rakte**	**rakt**	pass
smøre	**smører**	**smurte**	**smurt**	smear
spørge	**spørger**	**spurgte**	**spurgt**	ask
strække	**strækker**	**strakte**	**strakt**	stretch
sælge	**sælger**	**solgte**	**solgt**	sell
sætte	**sætter**	**satte**	**sat**	place
træde	**træder**	**trådte**	**trådt**	step
tælle	**tæller**	**talte**	**talt**	count
vælge	**vælger**	**valgte**	**valgt**	choose

The **g** in **-lg** and **-rg** is dropped in the pronunciation of the past tense of the following verbs:

følge – **fulgte**; **sælge** – **solgte**; **vælge** – **valgte**; **spørge** – **spurgte**

6 Two irregular verbs:

bringe	**bringer**	**bragte**	**bragt**	bring
vide	**ved**	**vidste**	**vidst**	know

7 Some verbs have vowel shortening in the past tense, e.g.:

bruger – **brugte**, use; **køber** – **købte**, buy; **træde** – **trådte**, step

82   THIRD CONJUGATION

1 A small group of verbs add the ending **-de** in the past tense:

Infinitive	Present	Past	Past Participle	Meaning
dø	**dør**	**døde**	**død**	die
have	**har**	**havde**	**haft**	have

2 The following have both **-de** and vowel change:

gøre	**gøre**	**gjorde**	**gjort**	do
lægge	**lægger**	**lagde**	**lagt**	lay, put
sige	**siger**	**sagde**	**sagt**	say

3 Two modal verbs are included here:

burde	**bør**	**burde**	**burdet**	ought to
turde	**tør**	**turde**	**turdet**	dare

83   FOURTH CONJUGATION – INTRODUCTION

This conjugation includes about 120 strong verbs, i.e. those whose past tense is monosyllabic (except in compound verbs) and formed either by **zero**-ending and (usually) vowel change or (in a few verbs) by adding the ending **-t** to the stem, with or without vowel change. The vowel change often (but not always) applies to the past participle too, which may thus have (i) the stem vowel, (ii) the vowel of the past tense, or (iii) a vowel different from both the stem and the past tense.

Infinitive	Present	Past	Past participle	
-e/zero	-e(r)	zero/-t	+ e(t) (+/– vowel change)	
		(+/– vowel change)		
drikke	**drikker**	**drak**	**drukket**	drink
falde	**falder**	**faldt**	**faldet**	fall

Strong verbs are best learnt individually, but many follow the same vowel change sequence. These gradation series are shown below in alphabetical order. Weak alternative forms are given in brackets; note that these sometimes have a different meaning.

84 FOURTH CONJUGATION: STEM VOWEL IN -a-

Gradation series a-o-a:

Infinitive	Present	Past	Past participle	Meaning
drage	drager	drog	draget	drag, go
fare	farer	for	faret	hurry
		(farede)		
jage	jager	jog	jaget	hurry, thrust;
		(jagede)		hunt, chase
lade	lader	lod	ladet/ladt	let;
		(ladede)	(ladet)	load
tage	tager	tog	taget	take

85 FOURTH CONJUGATION: STEM VOWEL IN -e-

1 Gradation series e-a-e:

Infinitive	Present	Past	Past participle	Meaning
bede	beder	bad	bedt	ask, pray

2 Gradation series e-o-e:

Infinitive	Present	Past	Past participle	Meaning
le	ler	lo	le(e)t	laugh

3 Gradation series e-å-e:

Infinitive	Present	Past	Past participle	Meaning
se	ser	så	set	see, look

86 FOURTH CONJUGATION: STEM VOWEL IN -i-

Strong verbs with the stem vowel -i- make up the largest group. They comprise five gradation series:

1 Gradation series i-a-i:

Infinitive	Present	Past	Past participle	Meaning
briste	brister	brast	bristet	break, burst
		(bristede)		
gide	gider	gad	gidet	feel like
give	giver	gav	givet	give
klinge	klinger	klang	klinget	ring, sound
		(klingede)		
sidde	sidder	sad	siddet	sit
stinke	stinker	stank	stinket	stink
tie	tier	tav	tiet	be silent
		(tiede)		

2 Gradation series **i-a-u**:

Infinitive	Present	Past	Past participle	Meaning
binde	binder	bandt	bundet	bind, tie
drikke	drikker	drak	drukket	drink
finde	finder	fandt	fundet	find
rinde	rinder	randt	rundet (rindet)	pass, roll by
slippe	slipper	slap	sluppet	give up, let go
spinde	spinder	spandt	spundet	spin, weave
springe	springer	sprang	sprunget	jump, spring
stikke	stikker	stak	stukket	prick, stick
svinde	svinder	svandt	svundet	decrease
svinge	svinger	svang (svingede)	svunget (svinget)	swing
tvinde	tvinder	tvandt	tvundet	twine, twist
tvinge	tvinger	tvang	tvunget	force
vinde	vinder	vandt	vundet	win

3 Gradation series **i-e-e**:

Infinitive	Present	Past	Past participle	Meaning
blive	bliver	blev	blevet	be, become
drive	driver	drev	drevet	drive, idle
glide	glider	gled	gledet	glide, slide
gnide	gnider	gned	gnedet	rub
gribe	griber	greb	grebet	catch, seize
hive	hiver	hev	hevet	heave, pull
knibe	kniber	kneb	knebet	pinch
pibe	piber	peb	pebet	squeak
ride	rider	red	redet	ride
rive	river	rev	revet	scratch
skride	skrider	skred	skredet	slip, walk out
skrige	skriger	skreg	skreget	cry, shout
skrive	skriver	skrev	skrevet	write
slibe	sliber	sleb	slebet	grind
snige	sniger	sneg	sneget	sneak
stige	stiger	steg	steget	rise
svide	svider	sved	svedet	burn, singe
svige	sviger	sveg	sveget	betray
vige	viger	veg	veget	retreat, yield
vride	vrider	vred	vredet	wring

4 Gradation series **i-e-i**:

Infinitive	Present	Past	Past participle	Meaning
bide	bider	bed	bidt	bite
lide	lider	led	lidt	suffer
skide	skider	sked	skidt	shit
slide	slider	sled	slidt	toil, wear
smide	smider	smed	smidt	throw
stride	strider	stred	stridt	struggle

5 Gradation series **i-å-i**:
Notice that the stem consonant **-g-** is dropped in the past tense:

Infinitive	Present	Past	Past participle	Meaning
ligge	ligger	lå	ligget	lie (position)

87 FOURTH CONJUGATION: STEM VOWEL IN -y-

Strong verbs with the stem vowel **-y-** make up the second largest group. They comprise five gradation series, four of which change the vowel to **-ø-** in the past tense:

1 Gradation series **y-a-u**:

Infinitive	Present	Past	Past participle	Meaning
synge	synger	sang	sunget	sing
synke	synker	sank	sunket	sink

2 Gradation series **y-ø-o**:

Infinitive	Present	Past	Past participle	Meaning
fryse	fryser	frøs	frosset	freeze

3 Gradation series **y-ø-u**:

Infinitive	Present	Past	Past participle	Meaning
bryde	bryder	brød	brudt	break
byde	byder	bød	budt	bid, offer
fortryde	fortryder	fortrød	fortrudt	regret
skyde	skyder	skød	skudt	shoot

4 Gradation series **y-ø-y**:

Infinitive	Present	Past	Past participle	Meaning
betyde	betyder	betød	betydet	mean
flyde	flyder	fløy	flydt	flow
gyde	gyder	gød	gydt	pour, spawn
gyse	gyser	gøs (gyste)	gyst	shiver

Infinitive	Present	Past	Past participle	Meaning
lyde	lyder	lød	lydt	sound
nyde	nyder	nød	nydt	enjoy
nyse	nyser	nøs	nyst	sneeze
		(nyste)		
skryde	skryder	skrød	skrydet	brag, bray
		(skrydede)		
snyde	snyder	snød	snydt	cheat

5 Gradation series y-ø-ø. Note the change of consonant in **fløj/fløjet** and **løj/løjet**:

Infinitive	Present	Past	Past participle	Meaning
flyve	flyver	fløj	fløjet	fly
fyge	fyger	føg	føget	drift, sweep
krybe	kryber	krøb	krøbet	crawl, creep
lyve	lyver	løj	løjet	lie (deceive)
ryge	ryger	røg	røget	smoke
smyge	smyger	smøg	smøget	slide, slip
		(smygede)	(smyget)	
stryge	stryger	strøg	strøget	cancel, iron, stroke

88   FOURTH CONJUGATION: STEM VOWEL IN -æ-

Strong verbs with the stem vowel -æ- comprise six gradation series, but each series has very few members:

1 Gradation series **æ-a-a**:

Infinitive	Present	Past	Past participle	Meaning
gælde	gælder	gjaldt	gjaldt	apply, be
			(gældt)	valid

2 Gradation series **æ-a-u**:

Infinitive	Present	Past	Past participle	Meaning
hjælpe	hjælper	hjalp	hjulpet	help
sprække	sprækker	sprak	sprukket	crack
		(sprækkede)	(sprækket)	
træffe	træffer	traf	truffet	hit, meet
trække	trækker	trak	trukket	draw, pull

3 Gradation series **æ-a-æ**:
This gradation series has three members; note that 'intr' = intransitive, 'tr' = transitive (cf. 103). **Kvæde** is now old-fashioned and very rare. **Være** has an irregular present tense form:

Infinitive	Present	Past	Past participle	Meaning
hænge	hænger	hang (intr) (hængte) (tr)	hængt	hang
kvæde	kvæder	kvad	kvædet	chant, sing
være	er	var	været	be, exist

4 Gradation series æ-a-å:

Infinitive	Present	Past	Past participle	Meaning
bære	bærer	bar	båret	bear, carry
skære	skærer	skar	skåret	cut, slice
stjæle	stjæler	stjal	stjålet	steal

5 Gradation series æ-o-æ:

Infinitive	Present	Past	Past participle	Meaning
sværge	sværger	svor (sværgede)	svoret (sværget)	swear

6 Gradation series æ-å-æ:

Infinitive	Present	Past	Past participle	Meaning
æde	æder	åd	ædt	eat, gobble

89 FOURTH CONJUGATION: STEM VOWEL IN -å-

Strong verbs with the stem vowel -å- comprise two gradation series, each with two members. All four verbs are vowel stems:

1 Gradation series å-i-å:

Infinitive	Present	Past	Past participle	Meaning
få	får	fik	fået	get, have
gå	går	gik	gået	go, walk

2 Gradation series å-o-å:

Infinitive	Present	Past	Past participle	Meaning
slå	slår	slog	slået	beat, hit
stå	står	stod	stået	stand

90 FOURTH CONJUGATION: VERBS WITH THE SAME STEM VOWEL IN ALL FORMS

Seven strong verbs have the same stem vowel in all their forms. However, they belong to the fourth conjugation since they have a monosyllabic past tense form. There are five different stem vowels and two of the verbs add -t in the past tense:

Infinitive	Present	Past	Past participle	Meaning
1 Stem vowel **-a-**:				
falde	**falder**	**faldt**	**faldet**	fall
2 Stem vowel **-e-**:				
hedde	**hedder**	**hed**	**heddet**	be called
3 Stem vowel **-o-**:				
holde	**holder**	**holdt**	**holdt**	hold
komme	**kommer**	**kom**	**kommet**	come
sove	**sover**	**sov**	**sovet**	sleep
4 Stem vowel **-æ-**:				
græde	**græder**	**græd**	**grædt**	cry, weep
5 Stem vowel **-ø-**:				
løbe	**løber**	**løb**	**løbet**	run

91   INFINITIVE

1 Form:
The infinitive is formed in one of two ways:

	Stem	Infinitive	
Consonant stems: stem + **-e**	**leg**	**leg*e***	play
Vowel stems: stem + **zero**	**dø**	**dø**	die

The infinitive form is usually preceded by the infinitive marker **at** except after modal verbs, verbs of perception and the verbs **lade**, **bede**.

2 Use of the infinite without **at**:

(a) After the modal auxiliaries **burde**, **kunne**, **måtte**, **skulle**, **ville**:

| **Han kan ikke svømme.** | He can't swim. |
| **Jeg skal gå om to minutter.** | I have to go in two minutes. |

(b) After **bede**, **føle**, **høre**, **lade**, **se**; often in object + infinitive constructions:

| **Vi hørte ham skrige.** | We heard him cry out. |
| **Jeg så hende ankomme.** | I saw her arrive. |

(c) Before the second of two coordinated infinitives:

Hun lovede at komme og hjælpe mig.
She promised to come and help me.

(d) In a few idiomatic expressions after **få**:

| **Nu får vi se.** | We'll see about that. |

(e) Colloquially in prohibitions or warnings, especially to children:

Ikke kigge/røre/pille næse!   Don't look/touch/pick your nose!

(f) After the (semi-)modals **behøve**, **gide**, **turde**, usage may vary:

Du behøver ikke (at) gå.	You don't have to go.
Han gider ikke (at) rydde op.	He cannot be bothered to tidy up.
Jeg tør godt (at) springe ned.	I dare jump down.

3 Use of the infinite with **at**:

(a) In two-verb constructions (verb + **at** + infinitive) with verbs such as:

begynde, begin; **beslutte**, decide; **forstå**, understand; **forsøge**, try; **håbe**, hope; **lykkes**, succeed; **pleje**, usually do; **synes**, think; **vælge**, choose; **ønske**, want, wish

Jeg forsøgte at åbne døren.	I tried to open the door.
Hun valgte at blive hjemme.	She chose to stay at home.

(b) When the infinitive acts as subject, subject complement, object or prepositional complement, note that English often uses the gerund (i.e. '-ing' form) in such cases:

At høre musik er afslappende.   Listening to music is relaxing.
       S

Lykken er at spise godt.   Happiness is to eat well.
       SComp.

Jeg lærte at tale dansk i skolen.   I learnt to speak Danish at school.
       O

Han tænkte på at gå i teatret.   He thought of going to the theatre.
       Prep.Comp.

(c) When the infinitive is the complement of a noun or adjective:

Vil du have lidt vand at drikke?   Would you like some water to drink?

Denne bog er svær at forstå.   This book is difficult to understand.

(d) **for at** + infinitive indicates intention:

Hun gik ind for at hente en bog.	She went in to fetch a book.
Han kom for at tale med os.	He came to speak to us.

NB Danish does not allow a split infinitive, i.e. nothing can stand between **at** and the infinitive.

92   PAST PARTICIPLE

1 Form:

	Infinitive	Present	Past	Past participle	Meaning
				-et	
I	**gro**	**gror**	**groede**	**gro*et***	grow
	vente	**venter**	**ventede**	**vent*et***	wait
				-t	
II	**høre**	**hører**	**hørte**	**hør*t***	hear
	spørge	**spørger**	**spurgte**	**spurg*t***	ask
				-t (some exceptions)	
III	**lægge**	**lægger**	**lagde**	**lag*t***	lay, put
				-et	
IV	**hjælpe**	**hjælper**	**hjalp**	**hjulp*et***	help
	vinde	**vinder**	**vandt**	**vund*et***	win

Mostly **-t** after **-d**:   **-t**
  flyde   **flyder**   **flød**   **flyd*t***   flow

Notice that in Conjugation IV (strong verbs) the vowel in the past participle may be different from that in the past tense.

When used as an attributive adjective, the past participle adds an **-e** in the definite and/or plural form. Past participles ending in **-et** usually end in **-ede** in the definite and/or plural form:

> **en ønsket gave**, a desired present; **den/de ønskede gave(r)**, the desired present(s)

2 Verbal use:

The auxiliaries **have (har/havde)** or **være (er/var)** + the past participle form composite tenses (cf. **96–97**):

Susanne har skrevet en bog.	Susanne has written a book.
De havde set filmen.	They had seen the film.
Jeg er begyndt at lære fransk.	I have begun to learn French.
De var taget til Aarhus.	They had gone to Århus.

The past participle is also used with **blive** to form one of the passive constructions (cf. **105**):

> **Bilen blev standset af politiet.**   The car was stopped by the police.

3 Adjectival use:

After the auxiliary **være** and in attributive position before a noun, the past participle may function as an adjective (cf. **52.4**):

Huset er lejet.	The house is rented.
det lejede hus	the rented house

Bogen var udvalgt.	The book was selected.
den udvalgte bog	the selected book
Stillingen er opslået.	The position is advertised.
den opslåede stilling	the advertised position

When the past participle is in predicative position and has a plural subject, there can be some uncertainty about whether it should be inflected:

(a) Weak verbs – uninflected or **-ede/-e**?
The uninflected forms with the ending **-(e)t** inflect in the following ways:

Conjugation I: **-et → -ede**, e.g. **lejet → lejede**; **ventet → ventede**
Conjugation II + III: **-t → -te**, e.g. **kendt → kendte**; **vedlagt → vedlagte**

Both forms are found when denoting a state of affairs, but modern Danish increasingly prefers the uninflected form:

Husene er lejet/lejede.	The houses are rented.
Spillerne er kendt/kendte.	The players are (well-)known.
Checkene er vedlagt/vedlagte.	The cheques are enclosed.

When the participle is a complement after verbs other than **være**, the uninflected form is also generally preferred:

De løb forskrækket(/forskrækkede) bort.
They ran away frightened.

(b) Strong verbs – uninflected or **-en/-ne**?
In Conjugation IV, the uninflected forms inflect in the following ways:

Singular form ending in **-en**: **-en → -ne**, e.g. **stjålen → stjålne**
Singular form ending in **-et**: **-et → -ne/-ede**, e.g. **tvunget → tvungne**;
                                    opslået → opslåede
Singular form ending in **-t**:   **-t → -te**, e.g. **afbrudt → afbrudte**

Here too both forms are usually possible, but again with a growing preference for the uninflected form:

Bilen er stjålet (stjålen).	The car is stolen.
Cf. **en stjålet (stjålen) bil**	a stolen car
den stjålne bil	the stolen car
Stillingerne er opslået(/opslåede).	The positions are advertised.
Cf. **en opslået stilling**	an advertised position
den opslåede stilling	the advertised position
Forhandlingerne er afbrudt	The negotiations are interrupted.
(/afbrudte).	
Cf. **en afbrudt forhandling**	an interrupted negotiation
den afbrudte forhandling	the interrupted negotiation

(c) Only the uninflected form is used in the passive:

Husene er blevet lejet.
Bilerne er blevet stjålet.
Stillingerne er blevet opslået.

93 PRESENT PARTICIPLE

1 Form:
The present participle is formed by adding **-ende** to the verb stem:

I	**bo**ende	II	**kør**ende	III	**dø**ende	IV	**ligg**ende
	levende		**spis**ende		**sig**ende		**rid**ende

2 Verbal use:
The present participle is used much less as a verbal form in Danish than is the corresponding form with '-ing' in English. It occurs mainly:

(a) In verbs of motion, e.g. **cykle**, cycle; **gå**, walk; **køre**, drive; **løbe**, run; **springe**, jump; etc., or verbs of expression, e.g. **bande**, swear; **græde**, cry, weep; **le**, laugh; **råbe**, shout; **smile**, smile; etc., when they follow verbs of motion like: **gå**, walk; **komme**, come; **løbe**, run; etc.

Han gik bandende/smilende bort.   He walked away swearing/smiling.
De kom gående/kørende/løbende.   They came walking/driving/running.
Børnene løb grædende hjem.   The children ran home crying.

(b) In verbs of position, e.g. **hænge** hang; **ligge** lie; **sidde** sit; **stå** stand; etc., when they follow **blive**:

Hun blev liggende/siddende/stående.
She remained lying/sitting/standing.

(c) In verbs of position, e.g. **hænge**, hang; **ligge**, lie; **sidde**, sit; **stå**, stand; etc., when they follow **have** + object:

Han har sin frakke hængende i entreen.
He has his coat hanging in the hall.

Jeg havde min cykel stående i skuret.
I had my bike standing in the shed.

Note that Danish has no formal equivalent to the English continuous forms (cf. **94.1**):

She is reading the paper.   **Hun læser avisen.**
                             OR: **Hun ligger/sidder/står og læser avisen.**

3 Other uses:
The present participle can also function as one of the following word classes:

(a) An adjective:
This is by far the most frequent use of the present participle. It can occur in both attributive and predicative position:

Attributive:
Det var en rammende bemærkning.   It was an incisive remark.
Vi står over for et stigende problem.   We are faced with a growing
problem.

Predicative:
Hun er charmerende/irriterende.   She is charming/irritating.
Han blev efterhånden trættende.   He gradually became tiresome.

(b) A noun (see also **54**):
This is especially common when the participle denotes people charac-terised by some activity. Some participles can even appear with the indefinite (as well as the definite) article, which is very rare in English, e.g. **en døende**, a dying person; **en logerende**, a lodger; **en rejsende**, a traveller; **en studerende**, a student; etc.

But there are far more examples with the definite article both in the singular and in the plural, e.g. **de(n) ankommende**, the arriving person(s); **de(n) besøgende**, the visitor(s); **de(n) dansende**, the dancer(s); **de(n) gående**, the walking person(s); **de(n) pårørende**, the relative(s); **de(n) ventende**, the waiting person(s); etc.

Den besøgende var en ung dame.   The visitor was a young woman.
De pårørende blev underrettet.   The relatives were informed.

The present participle can also appear in the genitive:

de rejsendes baggage   the travellers' luggage

There are a few examples of neuter nouns:

et anliggende, a (business) matter; **et indestående**, a bank balance; etc.

(c) An adverb:
As an adverb, the present participle usually acts as an amplifier (cf. **109.2**) for an adjective:

Hans tænder er blændende hvide.   His teeth are dazzlingly white.
Det var brændende varmt i solen.   It was burning hot in the sun.
Hun sang imponerende godt.   She sang impressively well.

Very few present participle forms are adverbs proper, e.g. **udelukkende**, exclusively.

TENSES

94   PRESENT TENSE

The present tense expresses:

1 What is happening here and now (instantaneous present) (see also **93.2(c)**):

Hvad laver du, Lise?	What're you doing, Lise?
Jeg sidder og skriver.	I'm (sitting) writing.

Danish has no exact equivalent to the English continuous forms but, apart from the present tense, certain constructions are used to indicate an ongoing state or action, e.g.:

Jeg er i færd/gang med at skrive.	I'm writing.
Jeg er ved at lave mad.	I'm cooking.

2 Statements of general facts (timeless present):

Jorden kredser rundt om solen.	The Earth orbits the Sun.
København ligger på Sjælland.	Copenhagen is situated on Zealand.

3 What is often repeated (habitual present):

Om mandagen begynder vi kl. 8.	On Mondays we begin at 8 o'clock.
Hvert år rejser vi til Frankrig.	Every year we go to France.

4 Events in the (near) future:

I morgen rejser vi til England.	Tomorrow we are going to England.
Jeg kommer snart tilbage.	I'll soon be back.

5 Events in the past that are dramatised (historic or dramatic present):

I 1914 udbryder 1. verdenskrig.	In 1914 World War I breaks out.

95   PAST TENSE

The past tense expresses:

1 An action at a definite point in the past (without reference to 'now'):

(a) Past tense only:

Vi plantede et træ i haven.	We planted a tree in the garden.

(b) Often with a time marker:

For ti år siden boede jeg i Danmark.	Ten years ago I lived in Denmark.
Vi kom sent hjem i aftes.	We came home late last night.

2 What was often repeated in the past:

Vi gik tit på pub i England.   We often went to the pub in
England.

This is often rendered by **plejede at**, used to:

Vi plejede at gå ud om lørdagen.   We used to go out on Saturdays.

96   PERFECT TENSE

Transitive verbs plus intransitive verbs not expressing motion (including
have and **være**) use **har** + the past participle to form the perfect tense:

Jeg *har slået* græsset.   I have cut the grass.
Han *har haft* mange gæster.   He has had many guests.
Vi *har været* på Madeira.   We have been to Madeira.

Some intransitive verbs, primarily those expressing motion or change, use
er + the past participle:

Kufferten *er forsvundet*.   The suitcase has disappeared.
Hun *er kommet* hjem.   She has come home.
Hvad *er* der *sket*?   What has happened?
John *er blevet* sagfører.   John has become a lawyer.

Intransitive verbs expressing motion may occasionally express either an
action or a state of affairs:

Action: **Han *har gået* hele vejen.**   He has walked all the way.
State: **Nu *er* han *gået*.**   Now he has left.

Action: ***Har* du *flyttet* sofaen?**   Have you moved the sofa?
State: **De *er flyttet* til England.**   They have moved to England.

The perfect tense establishes a link between the past and the present.
This may take the following forms:

1 An action at an indeterminate time in the past, but seen from the
present:

Hun har besøgt sin bror i Kina.   She has visited her brother in China.
Han er begyndt at ryge igen.   He has started smoking again.

2 An action in the past that has consequences for the present:

Det har sneet hele natten.   It has snowed all night. (It's still
white.)
Der har været indbrud.   There has been a burglary. (Things
are missing.)

3 An action repeated in the past, but seen from the present:

Jeg har været i Sverige flere gange.
I have been in Sweden several times.

Vi har set mange film i år.
We have seen many films this year.

4 An action continuing from the past into the present – with a time adverbial:

Jeg har boet i Birkerød i ti år (og bor der endnu).
I have lived in Birkerød for ten years (and still live there).

Cf. **Jeg har boet i Birkerød (på et tidspunkt, men bor der ikke længere).**
I lived in Birkerød (at some stage but don't live there any longer).

5 An action in the (near) future expressed in a subordinate clause that will be completed before the action expressed in the main clause:

Når jeg har afsluttet bogen, tager vi på ferie.
When I have finished the book, we'll go on holiday.

97   PAST PERFECT TENSE

The past perfect (or pluperfect) tense is formed with **havde/var** + the past participle (cf. the perfect tense in **96**):

Han *havde spist* **da du ringede.** He had eaten when you phoned.
Mødet *var begyndt* **da vi kom.**   The meeting had started when we came.

The past perfect is used to express an action in the past that took place before another action indicated by the past tense:

Da jeg nåede derhen, *var* **bussen** *kørt.*
When I got there, the bus had gone.

Poul fortalte os at han *havde været* **syg.**
Poul told us that he had been ill.

The past perfect may also be used to describe hypothetical events:

Hvis du ikke *havde drukket* **så meget, kunne du have kørt hjem.**
If you hadn't drunk so much, you could have driven home. (But you have.)

Hun ville have hjulpet dig hvis du *havde bedt* **hende om det.**
She would have helped you if you had asked her. (But you haven't.)

98 FUTURE TENSE

Although there is no formal future tense in Danish (as there is in French, for example), the combination of **vil** + infinitive is the nearest equivalent and the most neutral way of expressing future reference:

Hvad *vil* **der** *ske*?   What will happen?
I næste uge *vil* **det** *være* **for sent.**   Next week will be too late.

However, the future may be expressed in other ways, too, notably the following:

1 **skal** + infinitive implies an arrangement or a promise. A directional adverbial may replace the infinitive to denote an arrangement. Note that a promise usually has a first person subject and often includes the modal adverb **nok** as an extra assurance:

Vi skal mødes i biografen.   We are meeting at the cinema.
Han skal til Falster på søndag.   He's going to Falster on Sunday.
Jeg skal nok sende pengene i dag.   I'll send the money today.

2 Present tense with time adverbial:
It is more common in Danish than in English to use the present tense with future meaning. This often, but not always, refers to the near future:

Vi tager til Bornholm i næste uge.   We are going to Bornholm next week.
Om tre år går han på pension.   In three years he'll retire.

3 Present tense of **blive**, **få**, **komme**, often without a time adverbial:

Tror du det bliver kedeligt?   Do you think it will be boring?
Vi får godt vejr.   It's going to be nice weather.
Der kommer mange til festen.   A lot of people are coming to the party.

99 DIFFERENCES IN THE USE OF TENSES

1 Present tense in Danish – past tense in English:
In passive constructions when an action is completed but the result remains:

Bogen er skrevet i 1949.   The book was written in 1949.
Slottet er bygget i 1500-tallet.   The castle was built in the sixteenth century.
Hun er født i Nyborg.   She was born in Nyborg.

2 Present tense in Danish – perfect tense in English:

Er det første gang du er her?   Is it the first time you have been here?

3 Simple present tense in Danish – present continuous form in English:

Hvad laver børnene?	What are the children doing?
De (sidder og) ser fjernsyn.	They are (sitting) watching TV.

4 Past tense in Danish – present tense in English:
Especially to express spontaneous feelings (emotive past tense):

Det var synd for dig!	That's a pity for you!
Det var pænt af dig!	That's really nice of you!
Var der mere?	Is there anything else?

5 Perfect tense in Danish – past tense in English:
With emphasis on the result rather than the action:

Branner har skrevet *Rytteren*.	Branner wrote *The Riding Master*.
Din mor har ringet.	Your mother rang.
Hvor har du lært dansk?	Where did you learn Danish?

MOOD

100   MOOD AND MODAL VERBS

1 The attitude of the speaker to the activity expressed in the verb is indicated by:

Modal verb:	**Vi må løbe.**	We must run.
Imperative:	**Sov godt!**	Sleep well!
Subjunctive:	**Frederik længe leve!**	Long live Frederik!

2 Modal verbs have irregular forms, in particular the present tense:

Infinitive	*Present*	*Past*	*Past participle*	*Meaning*
burde	**bør**	**burde**	**burdet**	should, ought to
kunne	**kan**	**kunne**	**kunnet**	can
måtte	**må**	**måtte**	**måttet**	may, must
skulle	**skal**	**skulle**	**skullet**	must, shall
turde	**tør**	**turde**	**turdet**	dare
ville	**vil**	**ville**	**villet**	will, want to

3 Modal verbs also differ from other verbs in that:

- whereas other verbs only denote time/tense (past/present/future), the modals also express the speaker's own commitment or attitude to what is said;
- modal verbs are used as auxiliary verbs in two-verb constructions with a main verb in the infinitive:

Jeg _kan_ ikke _løbe_ længere. I can't run any further. (ability)
Det _må være_ det rigtige hus. It must be the right house. (logical necessity)

However, modals may also combine with a directional adverbial without an infinitive:

Nå, jeg _må hjem_ nu. Well, I'll have to go home now.
De _skal i biografen_ i aften. They are going to the cinema tonight.

4 Use of the modal verbs:

(a) **burde**:

probability
Ordet burde findes i ordbogen. The word ought to be in the dictionary.

strong recommendation
Du bør/burde se den forestilling. You ought to see that performance.

moral obligation
Man bør ikke lyve. One ought not to lie.

(b) **kunne**:

possibility, probability:
Hun kan være faret vild. She may have got lost.
Projektet kunne udføres. The project could be carried out.

permission, prohibition
Han kan (ikke) låne min bil. He can/can't borrow my car.

ability
Han kan ikke cykle. He can't (i.e. is not able to) ride a bike.

(c) **måtte**:

logical necessity
Hun må have glemt tasken der. She must have left her bag there.

hope
Må han dog snart få fred! May he soon be at peace!

permission, prohibition
Græsset må (ikke) betrædes. You may /must not/ walk on the grass.

command
Nu må du altså gå! You really must go now!

(d) **skulle**:

rumour
De skal være rejst til Spanien.   They are said to have gone to
Spain.

future in the past
Det skulle blive endnu værre.   Worse was to come.

arrangement
Vi skal mødes kl. 16.   We are going to meet at 4 pm.

promise
Det skal jeg nok sørge for.   I'll see to that.

command
Du skal gøre hvad jeg siger!   You must do what I tell you!

hypothetical
Hvis han skulle spørge dig ...   If he were to ask you ...

uncertainty
Hvad skal jeg gøre?   What shall I do?

Note also:

Vi skal lige til at spise.   We are about to eat.
Tak skal du have.   Thank you.

(e) **turde**:

idiomatic use
Det tør anses for sikkert at ...   It may safely be assumed that ...

bravery (= dare)
Han tør ikke sige sandheden.   He dare not tell the truth.

(f) **ville**:

future
Han vil være her om en halv time.   He will be here in half an hour.

volition
Jeg vil have en is!   I want an ice cream!
Jeg vil ikke bære tasken!   I won't carry the bag!

hypothetical
En gratis billet ville være dejligt!   A free ticket would be nice!

Note that **vil(le) gerne** corresponds to English 'would like to', and **vil(le)
hellere** to 'would rather'.

101   IMPERATIVE

1 Form: the imperative has the same form as the stem.

	Infinitive	Imperative
vowel stem	**gå**	**Gå!**
consonant stem	**standse**	**Stands!**
with double consonant	**komme**	**Kom!**

2 Use:

(a) The imperative is used to express a command, a request, a wish or a piece of advice:

Stop!	Stop!
Hent avisen!	Fetch the newspaper!
Hjælp mig et øjeblik!	Help me a moment!
Kør hellere lidt langsommere!	Better drive a little more slowly!
Sov godt!	Sleep well!

(b) All imperatives are technically second person, but the subject pronoun (**du**, **De** or **I**) is only occasionally made explicit, notably to express a contrast and in reflexive forms:

Sid du der, så laver jeg kaffe.	You sit there and I'll make the coffee.
Skynd dig/jer!	Hurry up!

(c) A command, etc., may be softened by adding adverbs such as **bare**, **lige**, etc.:

with **bare**:	**Gør du bare det!**	You just do that!
with **lige**:	**Giv mig lige bogen!**	Just hand me the book, please!

102   SUBJUNCTIVE

The present subjunctive form is identical to the form of the infinitive. It is rarely used nowadays and then only in a few fixed expressions:

Wishes:	**Gud velsigne dig!**	May God bless you!
	Ulrik længe leve!	Long live Ulrik!
Curses:	**Fanden tage ham!**	May the Devil take him!
Concessions:	**takket være hende**	thanks to her
	koste hvad det vil	whatever the cost

The subjunctive in unreal situations is often expressed by the use of **bare** or **gid** with the past tense:

Bare der snart skete noget!	If only something would happen soon!
Gid det var så vel!	If only it were like that!

Notice that English 'were' subjunctive is often the equivalent of Danish **var** indicative:

Hvis jeg var dig ...   If I were you ...

TYPES OF VERB

103   TRANSITIVE, INTRANSITIVE, COPULA AND REFLEXIVE VERBS

1 Transitive verbs have a direct object (DO):

Jakob købte en computer.   Jakob bought a computer.
          DO

Other transitive verbs: **gribe**, catch; **huske**, remember; **sige**, say; **tage**, take; **vide**, know; etc.
    Ditransitive verbs have both an indirect object (IO) and a direct object:

Pia gav Helle en gave.   Pia gave Helle a present.
    IO   DO

Other ditransitive verbs: **fortælle**, tell; **love**, promise; **låne**, lend; **meddele**, inform; **sende**, send; etc.

2 Intransitive verbs cannot have a direct object:

Den lille sover.   The baby is asleep.

Other intransitive verbs: **dø**, die; **græde**, weep; **fryse**, be cold, freeze; **lyve**, tell a lie; etc.
    Note, however, that some transitive verbs can be used intransitively, the object being latent:

Vi spiser [X] kl. 19. (e.g. **middag**)   We are eating [X] at 7 pm. (e.g. dinner)
Spørg [X] hvis du ikke forstår det.   Ask [X] if you don't understand it.

Other latent transitive verbs: **drikke**, drink; **hjælpe**, help; **tabe**, lose; **vaske**, wash; **vinde**, win; etc.

3 Some transitive/intransitive verbs in Danish exist in pairs:

Transitive	*Intransitive*
fælde, fell	**falde**, fall
lægge, lay, place	**ligge**, lie
stille, place (upright)	**stå**, stand
sænke, sink (e.g. a ship)	**synke**, sink (e.g. in the water)
sætte, set, place	**sidde**, sit

Note that in these pairs transitive verbs are usually weak and intransitive verbs strong. In one case both verbs are weak:

vække, wake (someone) up   **vågne**, wake up (of one's own accord)

4 Copula verbs are empty verbs that require a subject complement (adjective or noun) rather than an object to complete their meaning. The most common examples are **blive** and **være**:

Knud blev ingeniør.	Knud became an engineer.
De er meget venlige.	They are very kind.

Other copulas: **forblive**, remain; **forekomme**, seem; **lyde**, sound; **se ... ud**, appear; **synes**, seem; etc.

5 Reflexive verbs consist of verb + the appropriate reflexive pronoun; the latter functions as the object and agrees in form and meaning with the subject (cf. **67**, **70**):

Sonja gemte sig.	Sonja hid (herself).	(Reflexive)
Cf. **Sonja gemte pakken.**	Sonja hid the parcel.	(Object)

Other reflexive verbs: **barbere sig**, shave; **bevæge sig**, move; **glæde sig til**, look forward to; **opføre sig**, behave; **rede sig**, comb one's hair; **skynde sig**, hurry; **vaske sig**, wash (oneself); **vende sig**, turn around; etc.

(a) Many reflexive verbs in Danish are non-reflexive in English:

Du har forandret dig.	You have changed.
De giftede sig.	They (got) married.
Jeg kedede mig.	I was bored.
Hun satte sig.	She sat down.
Parret viste sig på balkonen.	The couple appear on the balcony.

(b) Many reflexive verbs express movement:

begive sig	set off
bevæge sig	move
bøje sig	bend
lægge sig	lie down
rejse sig	get up
sætte sig	sit down
vende sig	turn (round)

(c) The reflexive pronoun usually comes in the subject position (**n**) in the clause, but it follows any subject pronoun in that position (cf. **150**):

Gæsterne morede sig meget.	The guests enjoyed themselves a lot.
I aftes morede de sig ikke.	Last night they didn't enjoy themselves.

-s VERBS AND THE PASSIVE

104   -s FORMS, DEPONENT AND RECIPROCAL VERBS

1 Forms of **-s** verbs (for passive forms see **105**):

	Infinitive	Present	Past	Past participle	Meaning
I	**mindes**	**mindes**	**mindedes**	**mindedes**	recall
II	**synes**	**synes**	**syntes**	**syntes**	think
IV	**slås**	**slås**	**sloges**	**sloges**	fight

2 Uses:
There are three distinct uses:

- Deponent   **Det lykkedes ham at komme ind i huset.**
  He succeeded in getting into the house.

- Reciprocal   **Vi mødes ved rådhuset.**
  We'll meet at the town hall.

- Passive   **Middagen serveres kl. 19.** (See **105**.)
  Dinner is served at 7 pm.

3 Deponent verbs:
Deponent verbs are verbs that have passive form (i.e. **-s** form) but active meaning. Deponent verbs do not usually have a form without **-s**, unlike verbs in the passive.
Deponent verbs include:

fattes, be lacking; **findes**, be, exist; **færdes**, move, travel; **længes**, long; **lykkes**, succeed; **mindes**, recall; **mislykkes**, fail; **omgås**, mix with; **synes**, seem; **trives**, do well; **ældes**, age; etc.

4 Reciprocal verbs:
Reciprocal verbs usually (but not always) have a plural subject, and the individuals denoted by the subject each carry out the action simultaneously. Reciprocal action may also be expressed by using the reciprocal pronoun **hinanden**, each other (cf. **71**).

Vi ses i morgen.	We'll meet tomorrow.
De skiltes som gode venner.	They parted as good friends.
Han slås ofte med sin bror.	He often fights with his brother.

Reciprocal verbs include:

brydes, wrestle; **enes**, agree; **følges (ad)**, accompany (each other); **hjælpes ad**, help (each other); **mødes**, meet; **samles**, gather; **ses**, meet; **skiftes**, take turns; **skilles**, part, separate; **skændes**, quarrel; **slås**, fight; **tales ved**, talk; **træffes**, meet; **trættes**, quarrel; etc.

105   THE PASSIVE

1 Form of the **-s** passive:

	Infinitive	Present	Past	Past participle	Meaning
I cons	**ventes**	**ventes**	**ventedes**	–	be expected
I vowel	**ros**	**ros**	**roedes**	–	be rowed (of a boat)
II	**bruges**	**bruges**	**brugtes**	–	be used
III	**gøres**	**gøres**	**gjordes**	–	be done
IV	**ses**	**ses**	**sås**	–	be seen

Note that the **-s** passive does not normally have a past participle form; composite tenses are formed with the **blive** passive (see below).

2 Compare the following sentences:

Active clause	**Drengen**	**griber**	**bolden.**	The boy catches
	subject (agent)	active verb	object (patient)	the ball.

Passive clause	**Bolden**	**gribes**	**af drengen.**	The ball is caught
	subject (patient)	passive verb	prep. phrase (agent)	by the boy.

The transformation from an active to a passive clause involves three changes:

Active		*Passive*
object	→	subject
subject	→	(**af** +) prepositional complement
active verb form	→	passive verb form

However, the semantic roles of agent and patient remain unchanged, though the focus changes from agent to patient in the passive clause. Note that the passive transformation usually requires a transitive verb, but see (7) below.

The agent is often omitted in passive clauses when the person carrying out the action is either unknown or unimportant in the context:

Dørene åbnes kl. 20.	The doors open at 8 pm.
Ordet udtales med 'stød'.	The word is pronounced with a glottal stop.
Middagen serveredes i spisesalen.	Dinner was served in the dining hall.
Mødet blev holdt for lukkede døre.	The meeting was held behind closed doors.
Min bil er blevet stjålet.	My car has been stolen.

There are two main types of passive:

- **-s** passive: **Huset males.**   The house is (being) painted.
- **blive** passive: **Huset bliver malet.**   The house is (being) painted.

A third type also exists, however (expressing a state or result):

- **være** passive: **Huset er malet.**   The house is (now) painted.

3 Forms of the passive for **male** (paint):

	-s passive	*blive passive*
Infinitive	**(at) males**	**(at) blive malet**
Present	**males**	**bliver malet**
Past	**maledes**	**blev malet**
Perfect	–	**er blevet malet**
Past perfect	–	**var blevet malet**

4 The **-s** passive:
This is far less common than the **blive** passive. It is quite rare in the past tense and is virtually non-existent in the past participle. It is mainly used:

- in the infinitive with modal verbs that express notions such as obligation, permission, prohibition, volition, etc.:

Svaret bør sendes til kontoret.	The answer should be sent to the office.
Der må spises nu.	You may start eating now.
Græsset må ikke betrædes.	Do not walk on the grass.
Klagen skal undersøges.	The complaint has to be investigated.
Han vil klippes lige nu.	He wants to have his hair cut right now.

- in the present tense to express a habitual or repeated action (but see (5) below):

Lysene tændes kl. 21.	The lights go on at 9 pm.
Varerne bringes ud om fredagen.	The goods are delivered on Fridays.

Some verbs can only form the passive using **-s**, e.g.: **behøve**, need; **eje**, own; **have**, have; **skylde**, owe; **vide**, know.

- the **-s** passive can also occur in the past tense, but this use is very limited:

De ventedes først hjem kl. 21.	They were not expected home till 9 pm.
Han sås ofte på galopbanen.	He was often seen at the race-course.

5 The **blive** passive:

This is more common than the **-s** passive, and is the only option in the composite tenses. It is normally used:

- After modal verbs expressing possibility or future promise:

  Per kan blive udtaget til holdet.
  Per may be picked for the team. (It may happen.)

  Cf. **Per kan udtages til holdet.**
  Per can be picked for the team. (Nothing prevents it.)

  Bilen skal blive vasket i dag.
  The car will be washed today. (I promise it will be.)

  Cf. **Bilen skal vaskes i dag.**
  The car is to be washed today. (It has been arranged.)

  Hun vil blive forfremmet.
  She will be promoted. (It's certain.)

  Cf. **Hun vil forfremmes.**
  She wants to be promoted. (It's her wish.)

- To express a single action:

  Min søn er blevet inviteret ud.   My son has been invited out.
  Cf. **Min søn inviteres tit ud.**   My son is often invited out.

  Nu blev lysene tændt.   Now the lights came on.
  Cf. **Lysene tændes hver aften.**   The lights come on every evening.

Either the **-s** passive or the **blive** passive may be used to indicate a recurrent activity:

  Der stjæles biler hver dag./Der bliver stjålet biler hver dag.
  Cars are stolen every day.

6 The **være** passive:

(a) The participle is a verb:

Usually **være** + past participle indicates the result of an action, i.e. a state rather than an action:

  Bilen er vasket.   STATE/RESULT   The car is washed.
  Bilen er blevet vasket. ACTION   The car has been washed.

In the plural, the past participle form often remains unchanged (cf. **92**):

  Bilerne er vasket(/vaskede).   The cars are washed.

(b) The participle is an adjective:

The participle remains in the **-t** form in the singular irrespective of the gender of the noun, but inflects in the plural:

Pigen er forelsket.	The girl is in love.
Pigerne er forelskede.	The girls are in love.
Fordelen er begrænset.	The advantage is limited.
Fordelene er begrænsede.	The advantages are limited.

7 Impersonal passive constructions can, unlike all others, have either a transitive or an intransitive verb:

Der spises meget flæskekød i Danmark.
A lot of pork is eaten in Denmark.

Der blev talt meget om planen.
They talked much about the plan.

Der blev danset hele natten.
There was dancing all night.

COMPOUND VERBS

106   COMPOUND VERBS

1 There are two kinds of compound verb:

- Inseparable compounds in which the first element forms an integral part of the verb:

    Compare **tale**, speak; with **bagtale**, slander; **betale**, pay; **indtale**, record; **overtale**, persuade.

- Separable compounds in which the prefix may separate from the verb:

    (a) Where there is little or no difference in meaning between the compounded and separated forms:

    underskrive – skrive under   sign

    (b) Where there is a difference in meaning between the compounded and separated forms:

    udtale, pronounce   **tale ud**, finish speaking

2 Inseparable compounds include verbs compounded with:

nouns	**kæderyge**, chain smoke; **støvsuge**, vacuum clean
adjectives	**dybfryse**, deep-freeze; **renskrive**, make a fair copy

verbs	**sultestrejke**, be on hunger strike; **østregne**, pour with rain
numerals	**fir(e)doble**, quadruple
unstressed prefixes	**bedømme**, judge; **forblive**, remain
stressed prefixes	**anbefale**, recommend; **undslippe**, escape

3 Separable compounds include verbs compounded with:

stressed particles	**rejse** *bort*	go away
	svare *igen*	answer back
	stige *ned*	descend
	gøre *om*	repeat
	lukke *op*	open, unlock
	arbejde *over*	work overtime
	se ... ud	look

The particles are often prepositions or adverbs. Note that the stress is on the particle.

4 Some compound verbs exist in both the compounded and the separated form:

(a) With (virtually) the same meaning, the compounded form tends to be more formal:

afskære – skære af	cut off
deltage – tage del	take part
fastgøre – gøre fast	secure
fremrykke – rykke frem	advance
indsende – sende ind	send in
nedrive – rive ned	demolish
opgive – give op	give up
udvælge – vælge ud	select

(b) With different meaning, where the compounded form tends to have figurative/abstract meaning and the separated form literal meaning:

afsætte, remove, depose	**sætte af**, set down, take off
indse, realise	**se ind**, look into
oversætte, translate	**sætte over**, jump over, put (e.g. the kettle) on
understrege, emphasise	**strege under**, underline

7 ADVERBS

107 ADVERBS – FORM

Adverbs form a heterogeneous group, but the following are the major types:

1 Simple adverb:

> **aldrig**, never; **da**, then; **der**, there; **dog**, however; **her**, here; **ikke**, not; **jo**, you know; **just**, exactly; **kun**, only; **lidt**, somewhat, a little; **meget**, much, very; **netop**, exactly; **nok**, probably; **nu**, now; **næppe**, scarcely; **næsten**, almost; **ofte**, often; **straks**, immediately; **vel**, I suppose

2 Adverbs derived from other word classes:
Many adverbs derive from adjectives by adding the ending **-t** to the common gender singular form:

> **+ t   dejligt, dårligt, fint, godt, højt, langt, smukt**
> delightfully, badly, nicely, well, loudly, far, beautifully

The neuter singular form of the adjective is then identical with the adverb:

Hun gav et *højt* skrig fra sig.	**Hun skriger *højt*.**
She gave a loud shriek.	She shrieks loudly.
adjective	*adverb*

Other adverbs are derived from adjectives and other word classes through the addition of a variety of suffixes:

+ **deles**	**aldeles**, completely; **fremdeles**, still; **særdeles**, extremely
+ **ledes**	**anderledes**, different; **således**, thus
+ **mæssig(t)**	**forholdsmæssig(t)**, proportionately; **lovmæssig(t)**, legally; **regelmæssig(t)**, regularly
+ **s**	**dels**, partly; **ellers**, otherwise; **indendørs**, indoors; **udendørs**, out of doors
+ **sinde**	**ingensinde**, never; **nogensinde**, ever
+ **steds**	**andetsteds**, somewhere else; **intetsteds**, nowhere; **nogetsteds**, anywhere
+ **vis**	**heldigvis**, luckily; **muligvis**, possibly; **naturligvis**, naturally; **sandsynligvis**, probably

Both present and past participles (cf. **91f**) may also be used as adverbs:

forbavsende, amazingly; **overbevisende**, convincingly
begejstret, enthusiastically

Notes:

1 Adverbs derived from adjectives that do not take **-t** in their neuter singular form (cf. **46**, **48**) do not add **-t**, nor do the adverbs listed above ending in **-deles**, **-ledes**, **-s**, **-sinde**, **-steds**, **-vis** and those derived from participles. For adverbs ending in **-mæssig** the **-t** is optional but is normally added.

2 Adverbs derived from adjectives in **-(l)ig** add **-t** when modifying a verb (i.e. when used as adverbs of manner), but do not normally add **-t** when modifying other word classes (see amplifiers and diminishers in **109** below).

Hun spiller dejligt.	**Det var en dejlig varm sommer.**
She plays delightfully.	It was a delightfully hot summer.

3 Compound adverb:

alligevel, nevertheless; **altid**, always; **bagefter**, afterwards; **derfor**, therefore; **efterhånden**, gradually; **endnu**, still; **hidtil**, so far; **igen**, again; **måske**, perhaps; **også**, also; **rigtignok**, certainly; **simpelthen**, simply; **stadigvæk**, still; **vistnok**, probably

108 COMPARISON OF ADVERBS

1 Adverbs derived from adjectives have the same comparative and superlative forms as their adjectival counterparts, be they regular or irregular:

Positive	*Comparative*	*Superlative*	
dårligt	**dårligere/værre**	**dårligst/værst**	badly
godt	**bedre**	**bedst**	well
langt	**længere**	**længst**	far (of distance)
sent	**senere**	**senest**	late
tidligt	**tidligere**	**tidligst**	early

2 A few other adverbs compare as follows:

gerne	**hellere**	**helst**	willingly
længe	**længer(e)**	**længst**	for a long time
ofte	**oftere**	**oftest**	often
tit	**tiere**	**tiest**	often
vel	**bedre**	**bedst**	well

3 Adverbs ending in **-mæssig** and **-vis** do not normally compare.

4 Adverbs derived from present and past participles compare with **mere**, **mest**: **mere/mest overbevisende**, more/most convincingly.

109   USE OF ADVERBS

1 Adverbs may modify:

• a verb	**Han løber *hurtigt.***
	He runs fast.
• an adjective	**Damen er *utrolig* rig.**
	The lady is incredibly rich.
• an adverb	**Hun løber *forbavsende* hurtigt.**
	She runs amazingly fast.
• a clause	**Han er *ofte* hjemme.**
(see **145**)	He's often at home.

2 Amplifiers:
These are adverbs, especially those denoting degree or kind, that are used to amplify or strengthen the meaning of an adjective or another adverb:

alt for, far too; **ganske**, absolutely, quite; **meget**, very; **ret**, rather

Det er ganske rigtigt.
That's perfectly correct.

Han synger meget bedre end sin søster.
He sings much better than his sister.

Adverbs derived from adjectives are frequently used as amplifiers:

Det var en frygtelig kedelig film.
It was a dreadfully boring film.

Hun er en ualmindelig begavet studerende.
She's an unusually gifted student.

3 Diminishers:
By contrast, these are adverbs that are used to lessen or weaken the meaning of an adjective or another adverb:

dels, partly; **lidt**, (a) little; **nok**, enough; **næsten**, almost; **slet ikke**, not at all; **temmelig**, fairly, rather

Kan du køre lidt langsommere?
Can you drive a little more slowly?

Han var slet ikke glad for at være der.
He wasn't at all happy to be there.

110   ADVERBS INDICATING LOCATION AND MOTION

1 Danish adverbs of place show a distinction between motion and location which is now no longer found in English. One form (the shorter form) is found with verbs indicating motion towards a place and another (the

longer form) with verbs indicating location at a place. Compound adverbial forms expressing this distinction are also possible.

MOTION TOWARDS
Hun kom hjem.   She came home.
LOCATION
Hun er hjemme.   She is at home.

MOTION TOWARDS
Han går ud i haven.   He's going out into the garden.
LOCATION
Han går ude i haven.   He's walking in the garden.

2 The adverbs which have two forms in this way are:

Motion towards (Where to?) →•	*Location* (Where?) •	*Compounds*
bort (away)	**borte** (away)	
frem (forward)	**fremme** (forward)	
hjem (/to/ home)	**hjemme** (/at/ home)	**herhjem, derhjem** (here/there **herhjemme, derhjemme** at home)
ind (in)	**inde** (in(side))	**herind, derind** (in here/ **herinde, derinde** there)
ud (out)	**ude** (out(side))	**herud, derud** (out here/ **herude, derude** there)
op (up)	**oppe** (up)	**herop, derop** (up here/ **heroppe, deroppe** there)
ned (down)	**nede** (down)	**herned, derned,** (down here/ **hernede, dernede** there)
hen (over)	**henne** (over)	**herhen, derhen,** (over here/ **herhenne, derhenne** there)
om (over)	**omme** (over)	**herom, derom,** (over here/ **heromme, deromme** there)
over (over)	**ovre** (over)	**herover, derover,** (over here/ **herovre, derovre** there)

Examples of use:

Hvornår er vi fremme i Århus?   When will we get to Århus?
Hvornår når vi frem til Århus?   When will we get to Århus?

Bogen lå henne på bordet.   The book lay over on the table.
Læreren gik hen til bordet.   The teacher went over to the table.

Der er en have omme bag huset.   There is a garden behind the house.
De gik om bag huset.   They went behind the house.

111   SOME DIFFICULT ADVERBS

1 **gerne** 'willingly', etc.:

Jeg gør det gerne.	I'll willingly do it.
Jeg vil gerne have en øl.	I would like a beer, please.
Han læser gerne romaner.	He is fond of reading novels.
Det tror jeg gerne.	I'm fully prepared to believe it.

2 **ikke** 'not', 'no':

Jeg kender ham ikke.	I don't know him.
Han er ikke større end sin søster.	He's no bigger than his sister.

Ikke is also used, either on its own or together with **også** or **sandt**, as a 'question tag' following positive statements:

Vejret er koldt, ikke (også/sandt)?   The weather's cold, isn't it?

After negative statements, **vel** is used for this purpose instead:

Vejret var ikke koldt, vel?   The weather wasn't cold, was it?

3 **langt, længe**:
Both words originally derive from **lang**, but have different meanings:

langt, far	**længe**, for a long time
Er der langt til byen?	**Har I boet her længe?**
Is it far to town?	Have you lived here long?

4 **da**, **dog**, **jo**, **lige**, **nemlig**, **nok**, **nu**, **sgu**, **skam**, **vel**, **vist**:
These are unstressed modal adverbs expressing the speaker's attitude to what (s)he is saying, and it is difficult to give exact rules for their idiomatic use. Notice the following examples:

Det var da godt du kom.	**Du har da fået pengene?**
I'm very glad that you've come.	You have received the money, I hope?
Hvor er Karen dog rar!	**Hvorfor gjorde hun dog det?**
Karen really is a nice girl!	Why on earth did she do that?
Hun er jo syg i dag.	**Vil du lige holde mit glas?**
She's ill today, as you know.	Would you just hold my glass, please?
Han var nemlig meget rig.	**Han havde to biler, nemlig en Jaguar og en BMW.**
He was very rich, you see.	He had two cars: a Jaguar and a BMW.

Jeg tror nok vi vinder.
I think we'll probably win.

Det må du nok sige!
You can say that again!

Det er nu ikke rigtigt.
That's not right, you know.

Det ved jeg sgu ikke!
How the hell should I know!

Tom er skam i Odense.

Tom's in Odense, to be sure.

**Du har vel ikke et
     lommetørklæde?**
You haven't got a handkerchief
   by any chance?

Det mener du vel ikke?
You don't really mean that, do you?

Jeg var vist fuld i aftes.
I guess I was drunk last night.

8 PREPOSITIONS

112 PREPOSITIONS – INTRODUCTION

Prepositions are indeclinable words, i.e. they always have the same form. Prepositions usually govern a complement, and preposition + complement is called a prepositional phrase.

1 Types of preposition:
According to form, there are four types of preposition:

(a) Simple prepositions:
These consist of a single, indivisible word and include the most common prepositions, such as **af, efter, fra, i, med, på, til, ved**.

(b) Compound prepositions:
The preposition **i** may be prefixed to four other independent prepositions (**blandt, gennem, mellem, mod**) to form the compound prepositions: **iblandt, igennem, imellem, imod**, which are more formal variants of the simple ones. Note that **ifølge** (according to) is composed of a preposition + a noun.

(c) Complex prepositions:
These are made up of two or more words, including at least one preposition, which in terms of meaning form a unit. There are four main types:

(i) Adverb + preposition:
Together this combination indicates different types of direction or location. Note that some of the adverbs have a short form for direction/motion, e.g. **hen, ind, ned, op, ud**; and a long form for location, e.g. **henne, inde, nede, oppe, ude** (see also **110**). Thus:

> *Motion:*
> **Tina gik ud i haven.**   Tina went into the garden.
>
> *Location:*
> **Tina gik ude i haven.**   Tina walked (around) in the garden.

(ii) Preposition + noun + preposition:
As in English, there are numerous examples of this construction, e.g. **af frygt for**, for fear of; **i stedet for**, instead of; **med hensyn til**, as regards; **på grund af**, because of; **ved hjælp af**, by means of; etc.

(iii) Preposition + **og** + preposition:
These are most often opposites in meaning and thus contrastive, such as: **(stå) af og på (bussen)**, (get) on and off (the bus); **for og imod (forslaget)**, for and against (the proposal); **til og fra (arbejde)**, to and from (work); etc.

A few examples with **med** (with) as the second element can have a reinforcing effect, e.g. **fra og med (torsdag)**, from and including (Thursday); **til og med (i morgen)**, up to and including (tomorrow); etc. Note also: **i og med at . . .**, 'given the fact that . . .'.

(iv) Discontinuous prepositions:
In some cases the complement is surrounded or bracketed by two prepositions and the three elements form a prepositional phrase, i.e. the second preposition does not have a separate complement (unlike the examples in (ii) above). Examples: **ad (helvede) til**, like hell (*lit.* towards hell); **for (mange år) siden**, (many years) ago; **fra (nu) af**, from (now) onwards; etc.

2 Types of prepositional complement:

- a noun (phrase):

    De tog på *en lang ferie* med *børnene*.
    They went on a long holiday with the children.

    Vi gik rundt i *den dejlige, lille by*.
    We walked around in the lovely, little town.

- an object pronoun:

    Jeg boede hos *dem* i en uge.   I stayed with them for a week.

    Notice that after a preposition the pronoun in Danish, as in English, must be in the object form.

- an infinitive (phrase):

    Han gik uden *at sige noget*.
    He left without saying anything.

    Hun er bange for *at gå ud alene*.
    She's afraid of going out alone.

- a subordinate clause introduced by **at** or an interrogative word (a **hv-**word):

    Hun var sikker på *at hun havde ret*.
    She was sure that she was right.

    Hun er bange for *hvad der vil ske*.
    She's afraid of what will happen.

Notice that in English a preposition cannot govern a 'that' clause in this way.

- a prepositional phrase:

  Billetter kan bestilles fra *i dag,*
  Tickets may be booked from today,

  og de kan afhentes indtil *på fredag.*
  and they can be collected until Friday.

3 The position of prepositions:
Prepositions may adopt three different positions relative to the complement:

- before the complement (the vast majority of Danish prepositions do this):

fra hans mor	from his mother
i stuen	in the living room
med en kniv	with a knife
til Danmark	to Denmark

- after the complement (very few prepositions do this):

dagen igennem	throughout the day
Han blev natten over.	He stayed overnight/the night.

- bracketing the complement ('discontinuous') (see **112(c)(iv)**):

for ti år siden	ten years ago

On rare occasions a preposition forms a bracketing expression together with a noun:

for din skyld	for your sake
på firmaets vegne	on behalf of the firm

Notice that in Danish the preposition may be placed as the last element in a clause:

- in **hv-** questions (See **77**):

Hvad tænker du på?	What are you thinking about?

- in relative clauses (See **75–76**, **158**.):

  Det er hende (som) jeg drømmer om.
  She is the one that I dream of.

- when the prepositional complement occupies the topic position (**149**):

Ham kan man ikke stole på.	He's not to be relied on.
(Cf. **Man kan ikke stole på ham.**)	

- in infinitive phrases:

Her er noget at stå på.   Here's something to stand on.

4 Stressed and unstressed prepositions:

The most common monosyllabic prepositions (**ad, af, for, fra, hos, i, med, om, på, til, ved**) are unstressed when their complement is stressed, but stressed when their complement (usually a pronoun) is unstressed.

Stressed complement	*Unstressed complement*
Det var pænt af din 'ven at skrive.	**Det var pænt 'af ham at skrive.**
It was nice of your friend to write.	It was nice of him to write.
Jeg har ikke hørt fra min 'tante.	**Jeg har ikke hørt 'fra hende.**
I haven't heard from my aunt.	I haven't heard from her.

Another group of prepositions (**bag, efter, foran, forbi, før, (i)gennem, (i)mod, (i)mellem, inden, indtil, langs, omkring, over, siden, uden, under**), most of them having more than one syllable, are either stressed or unstressed when their complement is stressed, but stressed when their complement is unstressed.

Stressed complement	*Unstressed complement*
(')Bag 'huset stod der et stort træ.	**'Bag det stod der et stort træ.**
Behind the house was a big tree.	Behind it was a big tree.
(')Under 'broen løb en å.	**'Under den løb en å.**
Under the bridge ran a stream.	Under it ran a stream.

Prepositions placed after the complement and coordinated prepositions are always stressed:

Hun arbejdede natten i'gennem.   She worked throughout the night.
'Fra og 'med i dag er skolen lukket.   From today the school is closed.

Prepositions are stressed when their complement is omitted:

Han stod 'af [bussen] på hjørnet.   He got off [the bus] at the
corner.

113   THE MOST COMMON DANISH PREPOSITIONS

Below is a list of frequent Danish prepositions. Examples of common ways in which the twelve most frequent prepositions (asterisked) are used are given in paragraphs **114–26**. The remaining prepositions are used in much the same way as their English equivalents.

ad	by, at	***med**	with, by
*af	of, with, by	***om**	(a)round, about, in
bag(ved)	behind	**omkring**	(a)round
blandt	among	**over**	over, above, across
*efter	after, for	***på**	on, in, for
*for	before, in front of, at, for	**siden**	since
foran	in front of	***til**	until, to, for
forbi	past	**trods**	in spite of
for . . . siden	ago	**uden**	without
*fra	from	**uden for**	outside
før	before	***under**	under, below, during
hos	at (the home of)	***ved**	by, around
*i	in, on, for		
(i)gennem	through, by		
(i)mellem	between		
*(i)mod	to(wards), against		
langs	along		

Notes:

1 **ad** is used:

- together with an adverb to express direction/motion:

De gik hen ad gaden.	They walked along the street.
Børnene løb op ad trappen.	The children ran up the stairs.

- with the meaning 'in that direction':

De fløjtede/lo ad hende.	They whistled/laughed at her.

- with the meaning 'through an opening':

Jens kiggede ud ad vinduet.	Jens looked out of the window.

- with the meaning 'towards' + time:

Hen ad aften gik vi hjem.	Towards evening we went home.

Notice also: **en/to ad gangen**   one/two at a time

2 **forbi** means 'past' in a spatial sense:

Vi kørte forbi den nye bygning.	We drove past the new building.
Han smuttede forbi vagten.	He slipped past the guard.

3 **for . . . siden** corresponds to 'ago' and brackets the complement:

Vi mødtes for to år siden.	We met two years ago.

4 **hos** often corresponds to French *chez* and German *bei* (= at the place/home/work of):

Vi bor hos mine forældre. We're staying with my parents.
Han er hos tandlægen. He's at the dentist's.
Vi køber kød hos slagteren og frugt We buy meat at the butcher's and
   hos grønthandleren. fruit at the greengrocer's.

- as part of a lifestyle or culture:

Det er en gammel skik hos de indfødte. It's an old custom among the natives.

- as part of someone's character or work(s) of art:

Der er noget hos ham jeg ikke kan lide.
There's something about him I don't like.

Det er et hyppigt tema hos Carl Nielsen.
It's a frequent theme in Carl Nielsen.

5 **omkring** means 'about', '(a)round', 'circa', and is used in both a spatial and a temporal sense:

Der er en voldgrav omkring slottet. There's a moat around the castle.
Vi kommer omkring kl. 18. We'll be there around 6 pm.
Der var omkring 50.000 tilskuere. There were approximately 50,000
   spectators.

6 **siden** 'since' (see also **for ... siden** in (3) above):

Jeg har ikke set ham siden jul. I haven't seen him since Christmas.

7 **trods**:

Trods sin alder spiller han godt. Despite his age he plays well.

Notice also: **trods alt** 'after all', 'despite everything'.

114 AF

Af often denotes origin or source (though see also **fra** in **117**) and is used to indicate the passive agent (see **105**).

Agent	Material	Cause	Direction	Measure	Possession
by	of	from/of/ with	from/of/off	of	of

BY

Huset blev købt af en svensker. The house was bought by a Swede.
en roman (skrevet) af Herman a novel (written) by Herman Bang
  Bang
Musen blev fanget af katten. The mouse was caught by the cat.

OF

Huset er bygget af træ.	The house is built (out) of wood.
Han tog kammen op af lommen.	He took his comb out of his pocket.
dø af sorg	die of grief
ingen/nogle/de fleste/halvdelen af dem	none/some/most/half of them
ejeren af bilen	the owner of the car

FROM

Hun led af kræft.	She suffered from cancer.
Jeg købte computeren af ham.	I bought the computer from him.

WITH

Hun græd af glæde/skræk/smerte.	She cried with joy/fear/pain.

OFF

Han stod/sprang af bussen.	He got/jumped off the bus.

Notice also:

Pigen løb ud af huset.	The girl ran out of the house.
Manden stod op af sengen.	The man got out of bed.
fuld/træt af	full/tired of
ked af	bored with, sorry about

115   EFTER

Location/direction	*Time*	*Desire*	*Succession*	*Reference*
after/behind	after	for	after/by	according to

AFTER

Hunden løb efter børnene.	The dog ran after the children.
Efter lang tid kom brevet.	After a long time the letter arrived.
Kom efter kl. 16.	Come after 4 pm.
den ene efter den anden	one after the other

BEHIND

Luk døren efter dig!	Close the door behind you!
De stod efter os i køen.	They stood behind us in the queue.

BY

en efter en	one by one
spille efter gehør/reglerne	play by ear/the rules

FOR

Vi må ringe efter en taxa.	We'll have to ring for a taxi.
Damen spurgte efter Lise.	The lady asked for Lise.
lede/længes efter noget	look/long for something

ACCORDING TO

efter dansk lovgivning	according to Danish law
klæde sig efter årstiden	dress according to the season
Det går efter planen.	It is going according to plan.

Notice also:

høre efter	listen/pay attention to
lede/se efter	look for

116   FOR

For corresponds to English 'for' in a wide range of senses, but is only occasionally used with time expressions (but see **for . . . siden** in **112.3**, **113** Note 3):

Intention/purpose	*Indirect object*	*Cause/means*	*Place*
for	to	for	before

FOR

et program for børn	a programme for children
Jeg gjorde det for dig/for din skyld.	I did it for you/for your sake.
Tak for kortet/mad!	Thank you for your card/the food!
Han er berømt for det.	He is renowned/famous for that.
Vi købte fjernsynet for 4.000 kr.	We bought the TV for 4,000 DKr.
Hvad er det danske ord for 'goal'?	What's the Danish word for 'goal'?
for første gang	for the first time

TO

beskrive/forklare noget for nogen	describe/explain something to someone
Hun læste brevet højt for mig.	She read the letter aloud to me.
Det er nyt for mig!	That's news to me!

BEFORE

Vi har hele dagen for os.	We have the whole day before us.
Sagen kom for retten.	The case came before the court.

Note also:

for øjeblikket	at the moment
Hun er bange for edderkopper.	She's afraid of spiders.

Han interesserer sig for musik.	He's interested in music.
år for år	year by year
for det første/andet, etc.	in the first/second place, etc.
chefen for firmaet	the manager of the firm

and the following complex prepositions expressing position:

| **inden/uden for døren** | inside/outside the door |
| **oven/neden for trappen** | above/below the stairs |

for at + infinitive expresses intention:

| **Han tog til Norge for at stå på ski.** | He went to Norway to go skiing. |

117   FRA

Fra is used to suggest origin of space and time, as well as distance from a point.

Location	*Origin/source*	*Time*
from	from	from

FROM

Træet står en meter fra vejen.	The tree is a metre from the road.
toget fra Odense	the train from Odense
Hvornår flyttede du fra Ålborg?	When did you move from Ålborg?
Brevet er fra Dinah.	The letter is from Dinah.
fra september til december	from September to December
fra kl. 8 til kl. 12	from 8 till 12 am

Note also:

| **trække gardinerne fra** | draw back the curtains |
| **bortset fra** | apart from |

118   I

I is the most frequently occurring preposition and the second most frequent word in Danish, with many idiomatic uses beyond its basic meaning 'in'. With public buildings and places of work or entertainment, English 'in' is often rendered by Danish **på** (see **123, 129**). For the uses of **i** with expressions of time, see **128**.

Location/motion	*Material*	*Time when*	*Time duration*	*State*	*Frequency*
at/in/into	in	at/in	for	in	a/per

AT

Pia er i børnehave/kirke/skole.	Pia is at kindergarten/church/ school.
Toget standser i Roskilde.	The train stops at Roskilde.
i begyndelsen/starten/slutningen af maj	at the beginning/start/end of May
i fuld fart	at full speed

IN

Han arbejder i Paris.	He's working in Paris.
en statue i bronze	a statue in bronze
Det skete i april/i 1998.	It happened in April/in 1998.
i bilen/båden/glasset/huset/toget	in the car/boat/glass/house/train
være i form/i tvivl	be fit/in doubt

INTO (Motion is usually expressed by a directional adverb + **i**, see **110**.)

Han gik ind i køkkenet.	He went into the kitchen.
Hun løb ud i haven.	She ran into the garden.
Golfbolden trillede ned i hullet.	The golf ball rolled into the hole.

FOR

De blev der i fem uger.	They stayed there for five weeks.
Jeg har kendt ham i 30 år.	I've known him for 30 years.

TO

Skal du i biografen/teatret?	Are you going to the cinema/ theatre?
Klokken er fem minutter i ti.	It's five minutes to ten.

A/PER

en gang i minuttet/timen	once a minute/an hour
90 kilometer i timen	90 kilometres per hour

Notice also:

with parts of the body:

Jeg har ondt i hovedet/maven.	I have a headache/stomach ache.
Han vaskede sig i ansigtet.	He washed his face.

others:

Hun underviser i dansk.	She teaches Danish.
Glasset gik i stykker.	The glass broke.

119   MED

Med may be used to render most of the meanings of English 'with'.

Accompaniment	*Manner*	*Means*	*Possession*
with	by/in/with	with	with

WITH

Han rejste til Mallorca med Lene.   He went to Majorca with Lene.
Jeg drikker altid kaffe med fløde.   I always drink coffee with cream.
Hun sagde det med et smil.   She said it with a smile.
Spis ikke med fingrene!   Don't eat with your fingers!
Hvordan går det med dig?   How are things with you?
en mand med skæg/sort hår   a man with a beard/black hair

BY

De rejste med bus/fly/tog.   They travelled by bus/plane/train.
Vi sender en check med posten.   We will send a cheque by post.
Aktierne faldt/steg med 5 procent.   Shares fell/rose by 5 per cent.

IN

tale med lav stemme   speak in a low voice
Skriv ordet med store bogstaver!   Write the word in capital letters!

TO

Må jeg tale med chefen?   May I speak to the boss?

Note also:

Hun giftede sig med Anders.   She married Anders.
Lad være med at afbryde!   Stop interrupting!
Af med tøjet!/Ud med sproget!   Off with your clothes!/Out with it!

120   MOD

Direction	*Location*	*Time*	*Opposition*	*Comparison*
to(wards)	against	towards	against	against/compared to

TO(WARDS)

Familien kørte mod Esbjerg.   The family drove towards Esbjerg.
Toget mod Fyn er forsinket.   The train to/for Funen is delayed.
mod nord/syd/øst/vest   to(wards) the north/south/east/west
mod jul/påske/pinse   towards Christmas/Easter/Whitsun

AGAINST

Han stod lænet mod træet.   He stood leaning against the tree.

med ryggen mod muren	with one's back against the wall
De protesterede mod planen.	They protested against the plan.
Danmark skal spille mod Italien.	Denmark are playing against Italy.
mod mine principper/min vilje	against my principles/will

(COMPARED) TO

ti danskere mod seks finner	ten Danes compared to six Finns
tolv stemmer mod fem	twelve votes to five

121   OM

Om is used in a great many idiomatic senses, perhaps most frequently in certain expressions indicating future time (see **128.2** Note 1, **130**).

Location surrounding	Habitual time	Future time when	Subject matter	Frequency
(a)round	in/on	in	about/on	a/per

(A)ROUND

Hun havde et tørklæde om halsen.	She had a scarf round her neck.
De gik rundt om huset.	They walked round the house.

IN

om morgenen/eftermiddagen/ aftenen	in the mornings/afternoons/ evenings
om sommeren/vinteren	in summer/winter
De kommer om en uge.	They're coming in a week.
Om to år flytter vi til Spanien.	In two years we'll move to Spain.
Der er noget om snakken.	There is something in that.

ON

Vi spiser fisk om fredagen.	We eat fish on Fridays.
en afhandling om Holberg	a dissertation on Holberg

ABOUT

De snakker altid om tøj.	They always talk about clothes.
Bogen handler om et mord.	The book is about a murder.

A/PER

tre gange om dagen/ugen/året	three times a/per day/week/year

In certain instances, primarily with parts of the body, **om** is used colloquially without an English equivalent:

Han er kold/snavset om hænderne.	His hands are cold/dirty.

Notice also:

Vi bad om en øl.   We asked for a beer.

122 OVER

Location	*Motion*	*Time*	*Measure*	*List*
above, over	across, via	over, past	above, over	of

ABOVE

30 meter over havets overflade   30 metres above sea level
Lampen hænger over bordet.   The lamp hangs above the table.
Temperaturen er over frysepunktet. The temperature is above zero.

ACROSS

De cyklede over broen.   They cycled across the bridge.

OVER

Helikopteren fløj over byen.   The helicopter flew over the town.
over en femårs periode   over a five-year period
Over 40.000 så kampen.   Over 40,000 watched the match.

PAST

Klokken er ti minutter over tre.   It's ten past three.
Det er over midnat.   It's past midnight.

OF

et kort over England   a map of England
en liste over ansøgerne   a list of the applicants

Notice also:

Toget til Aarhus kører over Sorø.   The train to Aarhus goes via Sorø.
bekymret/overrasket/vred over   worried about/surprised/angry at
klage/vinde over   complain about/win against

123 PÅ

På is used in many idiomatic senses in addition to the basic meaning of 'on (top of)'. **På** is often used to render English 'in' in connection with public buildings and places of work or entertainment (see **129**). For uses of **på** with expressions of time, see **128**.

Location	*Direction*	*Time* when	*Time* duration	*Measure*	*Possession*
on/at/in	to	on	in	of	of

ON

Bladet ligger på bordet/gulvet.	The magazine is on the table/floor.
Vi tager til stranden i dag.	We are going to the seaside today.

AT

Vi mødtes på banegården/ biblioteket.	We met at the station/library.
Hun arbejder på universitetet.	She works at the university.
på bunden/hjørnet/toppen	at the bottom/corner/top

IN

Festen blev holdt på et hotel/en kro.	The party was held in a hotel/pub.
på gaden/himlen/marken	in the street/sky/field
Man kan gøre meget på kort tid.	You can do a lot in a short time.

TO

Jeg skal på kontoret/toilettet.	I'm going to the office/toilet.

OF

et barn på fire år	a child of four
navnet på byen	the name of the town
prisen på benzin	the price of petrol

Notice also:

på dansk/engelsk	in Danish/English
på denne måde	in this way
tro/tænke/vente på	believe (in)/think of/wait for
irriteret/sur/vred på	irritated/annoyed/angry with

124 TIL

Til often denotes motion towards a target, but it has several other uses, e.g. with the indirect object.

Motion	*Time when*	*Indirect object*	*Possession*	*'Intended for'*
to	till/until	for/to	of	for

TO

Han rejser snart til Amerika.	He's going to America soon.
fra ni til fem	from nine to five
Hvad sagde han til de andre?	What did he say to the others?
Jeg gav blomsterne til mor.	I gave the flowers to mum.

TILL/UNTIL

Kan du ikke blive her til mandag?	Can't you stay here until Monday?
Det må vente til næste uge.	It'll have to wait till next week.

FOR

Vi spiste fisk til frokost.	We had fish for lunch.
Han købte en bil til mig.	He bought a car for me.
Hvad brugte du hammeren til?	What did you use the hammer for?

OF

Han er forfatter til mange bøger.	He is the author of many books.
døren til soveværelset	the door of the bedroom

Remnants of old genitive endings in **-s** and **-e** are still found on nouns in some set phrases after **til**:

til bords, at/to the table; **til fods**, on foot; **til sengs**, to bed; **til søs**, at/to sea; **være til stede**, be present

Notice also:

til sidst/slut	finally
oversætte til	translate (in)to
vant til	used to

125   UNDER

Basically **under** corresponds to ideas expressed by English 'below', 'under(neath)', etc., but it is also used to render English 'during' in certain time expressions.

Location	*Motion*	*Time duration*	*Measure*	*Manner*
under/below/ beneath	under	during	below/under	beneath/under

UNDER

Katten sidder under bordet.	The cat is sitting under the table.
Bilen kørte under broen.	The car drove under the bridge.
børn under femten (år)	children under 15 (years old)
under ingen/disse omstændigheder	under no/these circumstances
Han gjorde det under protest.	He did it under protest.

BELOW

Temperaturen er under frysepunktet.	The temperature is below zero.
Det var et slag under bæltestedet.	That was hitting below the belt.

BENEATH

Det er under min værdighed.   It's beneath my dignity.

DURING (when used about a certain activity)

Der skete meget under krigen.   A lot happened during the war.
Jeg kedede mig under hans tale.   I was bored during his speech.

Notice also:

Under 20 personer mødte op.   Fewer than 20 people turned up.
under den forudsætning at   on condition that

126   VED

Ved suggests adjacency or proximity.

Location	*Time when*
at/by/near	about/around/at

AT

De sad ved bordet.   They sat at the table.
ved brylluppet/festen   at the wedding/party
ved solopgang/solnedgang   at sunrise/sunset
kærlighed ved første blik   love at first sight

BY

Vi har et sommerhus ved kysten.   We have a cottage by the coast.
Hun sidder ved vinduet.   She is sitting by the window.

NEAR

Louisiana ligger ved Humlebæk.   Louisiana is near Humlebæk.

ABOUT/AROUND

ved syvtiden   around seven (o'clock)

Notice also:

ved ankomsten/afrejsen   on arrival/on departure
slaget ved Hastings   the battle of Hastings
Der er noget mærkeligt ved hende.   There's something odd about her.

127   COMMON ENGLISH PREPOSITIONS AND THEIR DANISH EQUIVALENTS – SUMMARY

When translating English prepositional phrases into Danish, you may find the table below of help in choosing a suitable Danish equivalent.

	Time	Place	Manner	Subject matter	Indirect object	Agent	Measure
about	ved			om			
above		over					over
after	efter	(bag) efter					
across		over					
against		mod	mod				
around	omkring/ved	omkring					
at	i/til (128.1)	i/på/ved (129)					
before	før/inden	foran					
beneath		under	under				
below		under					under
by		ved (129.3)	med			af	
during	under						
for	i (128.4)				for/til		
from	fra	fra/af					
in	i (128.2)	i (129.1)	på				
into		ind i					
of	131	131		131			af/over/på
on	128.3	129.1, 129.2		om			
over	over	over					over
past	over	forbi					
through		gennem	gennem				
to	i	i/til			for/til		
under		under	under				under
with		hos	med				

128   TRANSLATING 'AT', 'IN', 'ON', ETC., AS EXPRESSIONS OF TIME

Because of the idiomatic nature of Danish prepositional expressions of time it is impossible to formulate rules which are both concise and one hundred per cent reliable. For the sake of brevity some variations have been deliberately omitted from what follows. The aim here is to present a scheme of basic conventions that applies in the majority of instances.

1 'At' + expressions of time:

'At' +	Festival	Clock
past	**sidste jul**	**klokken 10 (ti)**
habitual	**i julen**	**klokken 10 (ti)**
present	**i julen**	**klokken 10 (ti)**
future	**til jul**	**klokken 10 (ti)**

Notes:

1 **Sidste jul**, **i julen**, and **til jul**, render English 'at Christmas' = 'last Christmas', 'this Christmas' and 'next Christmas', respectively.

2 With year date expressions, Danish has either optional **i** plus end article (past) or **til** without article (future):

Det begyndte (i) julen 1998 og slutter til nytår 2008.
It began at Christmas 1998 and will end at New Year 2008.

2 'In' + expressions of time:

'In' +	Year	Decade/century	Month	Season
past	**i 1864**	**i 60'erne/i 1800-tallet**	**i april**	**i foråret**
habitual	–	–	**i april**	**om foråret**
present	–	**i 90'erne**	**i april**	**i foråret**
future	**(i) år 2020**	**i (20)20'erne**	**til april**	**til foråret**

Notes:

1 The preposition **om** (English 'in') answers the question 'When?' to express future action:

De rejser om en time/om en uge/   They're leaving in an hour/in a week/
om et par år.   in a couple of years.

2 The preposition **på** (English 'in') answers the question, 'How long does it/will it take?':

De kan køre til Møn på en time.   They can drive to Møn in an hour. OR:
     It'll take them an hour to drive to Møn.

I foråret/til foråret, etc., renders English 'in spring', etc. = 'last/this/next spring', etc.

3 'On' + expressions of time:

'On' +	Weekday	Date
past	**i søndags**	**den 1./første juli**
habitual	**om søndagen**	**den 1./første juli**
present	**(i dag)**	**den 1./første juli**
future	**på søndag**	**den 1./første juli**

Notes:

1 **I søndags** and **på søndag**, etc., render English 'on Sunday' = 'last Sunday' and 'this/next Sunday', etc., respectively.

2 For weekday + calendar date expressions, Danish usually has the weekday without the article and no preposition:

> **Han ankom torsdag den 1. april og rejser igen lørdag den 8. maj.**
> He arrived on Thursday 1 April and will leave again on Saturday 8 May.

4 'For' + duration:

Danish **i** + expression of time:

> **De har boet her i tre år.**   They've lived here for three years.
> **Jeg har ikke set hende i otte år/**   I haven't seen her for eight years/
>   **i lang tid.**   for a long time.

5 'During' = **under** (when the noun denotes an activity):

> **Han var pilot under krigen.**   He was a pilot during the war.
> **Hun fortalte os det under**   She told us during dinner.
>   **middagen.**

129   TRANSLATING 'AT', 'IN', 'ON', ETC., AS EXPRESSIONS OF PLACE

1 Because of the idiomatic usages of **i** and **på**, translation of 'at', 'in', 'on', etc., when expressing place relationships, is not always straightforward. The most common instances of Danish usage (to which there are exceptions) are set out below:

På (indicating 'on a surface')	*I (indicating 'inside')*
billedet på væggen	**et hul i væggen**
the picture on the wall	a hole in the wall
dugen på bordet	**dugen i skuffen**
the cloth on the table	the cloth in the drawer
et sår på læben	**et sår i munden**
a sore on the lip	a sore in the mouth
Hun sidder på en stol.	**Hun sidder i en stol.**
She's sitting on a(n upright) chair.	She's sitting in a(n arm)chair.
på Roskildevej	**i Bredgade**
skiven på telefonen	**tale i telefon**
the dial on the telephone	speak on the telephone
knappen på radioen/fjernsynet	**et program i radioen/fjernsynet**
the button on the radio/TV	a programme on radio/TV

2 Other uses of **på** and **i** to indicate location are:

rooms (dwellings)	rooms (spaces)
Han er oppe på værelset.	**Han kiggede ind i værelset.**

houses
Der står nr. 12 på huset.
It says no. 12 on the house.

houses
Der er mange mennesker i huset.
There are many people in the house.

areas of towns
på Vesterbro

towns
i Maribo

islands and small peninsulas
på Sjælland/Djursland

larger peninsulas
i Jylland

islands (non-independent countries)
på Færøerne/Grønland

countries (independent)
i Irland/Tyskland

continents (of one only)
på Antarktis

continents
i Afrika/Amerika/Asien/Europa

institutions
på biblioteket
på hospitalet
på universitetet

institutions
i børnehave(n)
i kirke(n)
i skole(n)

places of work
på arbejde(t)
på kontoret

places of entertainment
på diskoteket
på restaurant

places of entertainment
i biografen
i teatret

others
på stationen
på toilettet

others
i banken
i Brugsen/Illum (= stores)

3 Other Danish prepositions of location are:

(a) **hos** = at someone's house, certain places of work

Hun bor hos sine forældre.
hos bageren/tandlægen

She lives with her parents.
at the baker's/dentist's

(b) **ved** = at, by

Damen sad ved skrivebordet/vinduet.
The woman sat at the desk/by the window.

= by, on (with things extending lengthwise)

Familien bor ved floden/kysten/Øresund.
The family live by/on the river/coast/the Sound.

= near

Hotellet ligger ved jernbanestationen.
The hotel is near the railway station.

= of (with battles)

slaget ved Waterloo
the battle of Waterloo

130   PREPOSITIONS IN EXPRESSIONS OF TIME – SUMMARY

	Past	*Habitual*	*Present*	*Future*
Seasons				
forår, sommer	**sidste forår**	**om foråret**	**i foråret**	**til foråret**
efterår, vinter	last spring	in (the) spring	this spring	next spring
	i sommer/vinter			
	last summer/ winter			
Festivals				
jul, påske,	**sidste jul**	**i julen**	**i julen**	**til jul**
pinse	last Xmas	at Xmas	this Xmas	next Xmas
Days				
søndag,	**i går**		**i dag**	**i morgen**
mandag, etc.	yesterday		today	tomorrow
	i søndags	**om søndagen**	**i dag søndag**	**på/næste**
	last Sunday	on Sundays	today Sunday	**søndag**
				next Sunday
Parts of the day				
morgen,	**i morges**	**om morgenen**	**her/nu til morgen**	**i morgen tidlig**
formiddag	**i formiddags**	**om formiddagen**	**(her) i**	**i morgen**
	(earlier)	in the	**formiddag**	**formiddag**
	this morning	morning(s)	this morning	tomorrow morning
eftermiddag	**i eftermiddags**	**om efter-**	**(nu) i efter-**	**i morgen efter-**
	(earlier) this	**middagen**	**middag**	**middag**
	afternoon	in the afternoon(s)	this afternoon	tomorrow afternoon
aften	**i aftes**	**om aftenen**	**(nu) i aften**	**i morgen aften**
	last night/ evening	in the evening(s)	this evening	tomorrow evening
nat	**i nat**	**om natten**	**(her) i nat**	**i morgen nat**
	last night/during the night	at night	tonight	tomorrow night
Years, months				
år	**sidste år**	**om året**	**i år**	**(til) næste år**
	last year	per year	this year	next year
januar, etc.	**i/sidste januar**	**i januar**	**i januar**	**til januar**
	last January	in January	this January	next January

131   TRANSLATING 'OF'

The English preposition 'of' may be rendered in a great many ways in Danish. What follows is by no means a complete account, but it will provide guidance on how to translate 'of' in the most common instances.

1 Possessive 'of':

(a) English possessive 'of' is commonly rendered by Danish **-s** genitive (cf. **37**):

the owner of the car	**bilens ejer**
the roof of the church	**kirkens tag**
the top of the tree	**træets top**

(b) In many cases Danish prefers a compound noun:

the owner of the car/car owner	**bilejeren**
the roof of the church/church roof	**kirketaget**
the top of the tree/tree top	**trætoppen**

2 'The city of Roskilde', etc.:
When English 'of' may be replaced by commas indicating apposition, it is rendered without a preposition in Danish:

the city of Roskilde	**byen Roskilde**
the kingdom of Norway	**kongeriget Norge**
the Republic of Ireland	**republikken Irland**
the month of May	**maj måned**

3 'A cup of tea', etc.:
Expressions with 'of' denoting measure are usually rendered without a preposition in Danish:

a cup of tea	**en kop te**
a pair of shoes	**et par sko**
5 kilos of potatoes	**5 kilo kartofler**
a large number of Danes	**et stort antal danskere**

Notes:

1 'half of'/'part of'/'some of'/'the majority of':

half of/some of the book	**halvdelen af/en del/noget af bogen**
some/the majority of the voters	**nogle/flertallet af vælgerne**

2 Danish usually has **på** corresponding to English 'of' when it is followed by a number:

a salary of 300,000 kroner	**en løn på 300.000 kroner**
a woman of forty	**en kvinde på fyrre år**

4 Dates:

Danish has no preposition for 'of' when it is used in dates:

the 1st/first of January **den 1./første januar**
in May of 1956 **i maj 1956**

5 'A heart of stone', etc.:

'Of' indicating material is rendered by **af** in Danish (cf. **114**):

a heart of stone **et hjerte af sten**
a statue of marble **en statue af marmor**

6 'The Queen of Denmark', etc.:

'Of' denoting representation or origin may be rendered by Danish **af** or **fra**. (The sense of geographical origin is stronger with **fra**):

the Queen of Denmark **dronningen af Danmark**
 (= Danmarks dronning)

a young man of Jutland **en ung mand fra Jylland**
 (= en ung jyde)

Notice that where 'of' = 'in', Danish has **i**:

the mayor of Helsingør **borgmesteren i Helsingør**
The Merchant of Venice **Købmanden i Venedig**

7 'North of', etc.:

'Of' with compass points = **for**:

north of Skagen **nord for Skagen**

Note: the north of England **Nordengland**

8 'A map of Greenland', etc.:

With maps, lists and directories, **over** is often used:

a map of Greenland **et kort over Grønland**
a list of telephone numbers **en liste over telefonnumre**
a survey of Danish towns **en oversigt over danske byer**

9 'A professor of law', etc.:

With job titles, **i** is normally used:

a professor of law **en professor i jura**
 (= en juraprofessor)

a teacher of English **en lærer i engelsk**
 (= en engelsklærer)

9 INTERJECTIONS

1 Introduction
There are two types of interjection, both of which chiefly belong to the spoken language. They usually appear at the beginning of a sentence and are separated from the rest of it by a comma. Type 1 includes exclamations and spontaneous expressions of feelings (e.g. discomfort, joy, etc.) without any reference, and imitations of sounds, while Type 2 consists of formulaic words and expressions used in conventional situations (e.g. affirmations, denials, greetings, etc.).

Type 1:

2 Exclamations, expressions of feelings:

(a) Positive feelings:
Delight, satisfaction: **ih**, **åh**:

Ih, hvor er hun sød!	Oh, isn't she sweet?
Åh, hvor er det dejligt!	Oh, isn't it lovely?

Praise, joy, excitement: **bravo**, **hurra**, **juhu**:

Bravo, det var flot klaret!	Bravo, well done!
Hurra, vi har vundet i tips!	Hurrah, we've won the pools!
Juhu, vi skal i Tivoli i aften!	Yippee, we are going to Tivoli tonight!

Surprise: **hovsa**, **ih**, **nej**, **nå**:

Hovsa, jeg havde ikke set dig!	Whoops, I hadn't seen you!
Ih/Nej, sikke en overraskelse!	Oh, what a surprise!
Nå, jeg troede det var i morgen!	Oh, I thought it was tomorrow!

(b) Negative feelings:
Annoyance: **årh**:

Årh, nu gik det lige så godt!	Oh no, and it was going so well!
Øv, hvorfor må jeg ikke det?	Oh, why can't I do that?

Disapproval, disgust, discomfort: **fy, føj, puh(a)**:

Fy, hvor skulle du skamme dig!	Shame on you!
Føj, hvor ser den ækel ud!	Ugh, doesn't it look nasty!
Puh, hvor er det varmt!	Phew, it's hot!
Puha, hvor her lugter!	Pooh, it smells in here!

Fear: **ih, nej, uh(a)**:

Ih/Nej/Uh, hvor blev jeg bange!	Oh, I was really scared!
Uha, hvor er her mørkt!	Gosh, isn't it dark in here!

Hesitation: **øh**:

Øh, det ved jeg faktisk ikke.	Er, I don't really know.

Pain: **av**:

Av, hvor gør det ondt!	Ow, it hurts!

3 Imitations of sounds (onomatopoeia):
Sounds of animals: **miav** (cat); **muh** (cow); **mæh** (sheep); **pruh** (horse); **vov** (dog); **øf** (pig).
Sounds of objects: **bang** (door, gun); **ding-dong** (bell); **plask** (into water); **tik-tak** (clock).

4 Commands to animals and people (a mixture of Type 1 and Type 2):
Animals: to dogs: **Dæk!**, Down!; to horses: **Hyp! Prr!**, Gee up! Whoah!;
People: to children: **Hys! Ssh!**, Hush! Ssh!; to soldiers: **Giv agt!**, Ready!;
Ret!, Attention!.

Type 2:

5 Affirmations: **ja**, **jo** and their compound forms:

(a) **Ja, jo** (**jo** is used in the answer when the question contains a negation):

Har du set min nye bil?	**Ja./Ja, det har jeg.**
Have you seen my new car?	Yes./Yes, I have.
Er du ikke træt?	**Jo./Jo, det er jeg.**
Aren't you tired?	Yes./Yes, I am.
Har du aldrig været i New York?	**Jo, to gange.**
Have you never been to New York?	Yes, twice.

(b) **Javist, jovist** (stronger affirmation, greater assurance):

Tror du at han stadig elsker mig?	**Javist gør han det!**
Do you think he still loves me?	Of course he does!

Har du ikke vandet blomsterne? **Jovist har jeg så!**
Haven't you watered the flowers? Yes, I certainly have!

(c) **Jamen** (expresses mild protest or sympathy):

De skal snart giftes. **Jamen, de er da alt for unge!**
They are getting married soon. But they are far too young!

Jamen dog, har du slået dig? Oh dear, have you hurt yourself?

(d) **Jaså** (signals surprise and often disapproval):

Hun er begyndt at arbejde igen. **Jaså, det havde jeg nu ikke ventet!**
She has started to work again. Really, I hadn't expected that!

Jeg har glemt at købe løg. **Jaså, så må vi jo klare os uden!**
I have forgotten to buy onions. Well then, we'll have to do without.

(e) **Javel** (denotes acceptance of a statement or an order):

Hun kommer ikke til mødet. **Javel, det skal jeg notere.**
She's not coming to the meeting. OK, I'll make a note of that.

Ti stille når jeg taler! **Javel, hr. sergeant!**
Shut up when I'm talking! Yes, sir! (i.e. a sergeant)

6 Denials:

(a) **Nej** (clear denial or refusal):

Kunne du lide filmen? **Nej, jeg syntes den var kedelig.**
Did you like the film? No, I thought it was boring.

Har du tid et øjeblik? **Nej./Nej, det har jeg ikke.**
Have you got a moment? No./No, I haven't.

(b) **Næ(h)** (implies doubt or hesitation):

Tror du han tog pengene? **Næh, men man ved jo aldrig!**
Do you think he took the money? Well no, but you never know!

7 Uncertainty: **Tja(h)** (somewhere in between 'yes' and 'no'):

Tror du vi vinder i aften? **Tjah, måske, vi har da en chance.**
Do you think we'll win tonight? Well, perhaps, we've got a chance.

8 Greetings and exhortations:

(a) On meeting: **dav(s)**, **godaften**, **goddag**, **goddav(s)**, **godmorgen**, **hej**.

(b) On parting: **farvel**, **hej**, **på gensyn**.

(c) Seasonal: **glædelig jul**, Merry Christmas; **godt nytår**, Happy New Year; **god påske**, Happy Easter; **til lykke/tillykke med fødselsdagen**, happy birthday.

(d) Thanks: **(mange) tak**, (many) thanks; **tak for mad/sidst**, thanks for the food/the last time we met; **selv tak/tak i lige måde**, thank you (in return).

(e) Apologies and responses: **om forladelse**, sorry; **undskyld**, excuse me/sorry; **åh, jeg be'r/ingen årsag/det var så lidt**, not at all/don't mention it.

(f) Others: **skål**, cheers; **værsgo**, here you are.

9 Expletives (mostly names for God, the Devil, diseases and excrement):

fandens/helvedes/satans (også), for fanden/helvede/satan, kraftedeme, lort, pis, sateme, sgu, skid, skide- (as a prefix used for extra emphasis, e.g. **skidegod, skidesød**, etc.), **ved gud**

Euphemisms: **for katten/pokker/søren, pokkers, skam, søreme**.

10 CONJUNCTIONS

133 COORDINATING CONJUNCTIONS

1 These join clauses or elements of the same kind and are always found between the words or groups of words that they link (see **140**). They do not affect the word order within the groups of words that they link.

Coordination (linking) of:

two subjects	***Tom og Jannie* taler med børnene.**
	Tom and Jannie are talking to the children.
two verbs	**De *sidder* og *leger.***
	They are sitting playing.
two main clauses	**Jeg holder af Anders, og *han holder af mig.***
(straight word order)	I'm fond of Anders, and he's fond of me.
two main clauses	***Ham kan jeg godt lide*, og *det kan hun også.***
(inverted word order)	I like him and she does, too.
two subordinate clauses	**Jeg håber *at han vinder*, og *at han sætter ny rekord.***
	I hope that he wins and that he sets a new record.

2 Coordinating conjunctions include:

og **Gå hjem og sov!** and
Go home and go to sleep!

eller **Pengene eller livet!** or
Your money or your life!

for **Han løb hurtigt, for han havde travlt.** for, because
He ran quickly for he was in a hurry.

men **Jeg vasker op, men min kone sørger for maden.** but
I do the washing up but my wife does the cooking.

så **Hun plaskede i vandet, så alle blev våde.** so
She splashed in the water so they all got wet.

134 SUBORDINATING CONJUNCTIONS

1 These link main clauses (MC) and subordinate clauses (SC). Subordinate clauses may follow or precede the main clause:

Cf. ***De sover når de er trætte.***   They sleep when they're tired.
MC   /sub + SC
        conj

Når de er trætte, sover de.   When they're tired they sleep.
sub + SC   /MC
conj

2 Subordinating conjunctions and other words (listed below) which introduce subordinate clauses will occupy the first position in the subordinate clause and may affect the word order in those clauses (see **156**, **159**). Such words are of two main types:

(a) General subordinators:
These words introduce indirect speech (**at** = that) and indirect yes/no questions (**om** = whether, if), but impart no meaning to the clause, unlike other subordinating conjunctions in 2(b) below. Just as in English, **at** may sometimes be omitted:

at   **Hun sagde (at) hun arbejdede for hårdt.**   that
     She said (that) she was working too hard.
     (Cf. direct speech: **Hun sagde: 'Jeg arbejder for hårdt.'**)

om   **Jeg spurgte om hun arbejdede for hårdt.**   whether, if
     I asked whether she was working too hard.
     (Cf. direct question: **Jeg spurgte: 'Arbejder du for hårdt?'**)

(b) Other subordinating conjunctions:
These words introduce different kinds of adverbial clause (cf. **156**, **159**):

(i) Time:

***Når* du får tid, kan du slå græsset.**   when
When you get the time, you can cut the grass.

***Når* vi var hjemme, plejede far at gå ud.**   when(ever)
Whenever we were at home Dad used to go out.

***Da* vi kom hjem, var han gået ud.**   when
When we came home, he'd gone out.

Jeg er blevet professor *siden* vi sidst sås.   since
I've become a professor since we last met.

***Me(de)ns* jeg henter flasken, kan du finde nogle glas.**   while
While I get the bottle, you can find some glasses.

***Inden* jeg nåede frem, var det for sent.**   before
Before I got there, it was too late.

Note: **Når** (when) is used to introduce clauses describing present and future events, and for repeated actions in the past (= whenever). **Da** (when) is used about a single event or occasion which took place in the past.

(ii) Cause:

Han kommer ikke i dag *fordi* **han er syg.** He's not coming today because he's ill.	because
Eftersom **det er påskedag, holder butikkerne lukket.** Because it's Easter Sunday, the shops are closed.	because
Vi kom sent hjem *da* **toget var forsinket.** We got home late as the train was delayed.	as
Siden **du spørger så pænt, skal du få svar.** Since you ask so nicely, you'll get an answer.	since

(iii) Condition:

Hvis **det bliver ved med at sne, kan vi stå på ski.** If it carries on snowing we can go skiing.	if
Jeg kommer *hvis* **jeg får tid.** I'll come if I get the time.	if
Bare **jeg ser et glas vand, bliver jeg søsyg.** If I just see a glass of water I get seasick.	if only/just

(iv) Concession:

Hun frøs *selvom* **hun havde frakke på.** She was cold even though she was wearing a coat.	(al)though/ even though
Han sagde nej *skønt* **han mente jo.** He said no though he meant yes.	(al)though/ even though

(v) Intention:

De gjorde meget *for at* **han skulle føle sig hjemme.** They did a lot to make him feel at home.	(in order) to
Han gemte sig *så (at)* **de ikke ville få øje på ham.** He hid so that they wouldn't see him.	so that

(vi) Result:

Det var *så* **koldt** *at* **søen frøs til.** It was so cold that the lake froze over.	so ... that

(vii) Comparison:

Anna er lige *så* stor *som* sin søster/*som* hendes søster er.   as ... as ...
Anna is just as big as her sister/as her sister is.

Søren er større *end* sin bror/*end* hans bror er.   than
Søren is bigger than his brother/than his brother is.

***Jo* mere det sner, *jo* gladere bliver børnene.**   the ... the ...
The more it snows, the happier are the children.

***Jo* længere vi venter, *desto* sværere bliver det at få det sagt.**   the ... the ...
The longer we wait, the harder it becomes to say it.

135   OTHER SUBORDINATORS

These are words which are not conjunctions, but nevertheless introduce subordinate clauses.

1 Interrogative pronouns (**hv-** words) and adverbs (cf. **77**, **107**):
These words introduce indirect **hv-** questions (cf. **138–39**):

Ved du *hvad* han gjorde?   Do you know what he did?
Kan du sige mig *hvem* hun er?   Can you tell me who she is?
Ved du *hvordan* han har det,   Do you know how he is and when
    og *hvornår* han kommer?   he's coming?

When **hvad** and **hvem** are the subject of a subordinate clause, **der** is introduced as a subject marker:

Han vidste ikke hvem *der* havde gjort det.
He didn't know who had done it.

Hun kunne ikke fortælle mig hvad *der* var sket.
She couldn't tell me what had happened.

2 Relative pronouns and adverbs (cf. **75–76**, **107**):
These words introduce relative clauses (cf. **154.2**), which usually form attributes to subjects, objects or complements:

Vi har fået en ny lærer *der* er meget dygtig.
We have got a teacher who's very good.

Der er noget *som* jeg må tale med dig om.
There's something I need to talk to you about.

136   TRANSLATING SOME DIFFICULT CONJUNCTIONS

1 'After' is a preposition, adverb and conjunction in English. **Efter** is an adverb and a preposition but not a conjunction (though it is increasingly being perceived as such in modern Danish), and therefore cannot normally introduce a subordinate clause unless it is followed by **at**:

The house burnt down shortly after they left.
Huset brændte kort *efter at* **de var rejst.**

2 'As' = 'for' = **for**:

He handed in his notice as he couldn't take the pressure.
Han sagde op, for han kunne ikke klare presset.

= 'while' = **mens (medens)**, **idet**:

As he was talking he went red in the face.
Mens han talte, blev han rød i hovedet.

= 'because' = **fordi** (in written language also **da**, **eftersom**):

We went home again straightaway because the weather was bad.
Vi tog straks hjem igen fordi vejret var dårligt.

3 'As ... as' in comparisons = **(lige) så ... som**:

He is as tall as his father/as his father is.
Han er (lige) så høj som sin far/som hans far er.

4 'Before' = **inden, før**:

I'd like to be told before you leave.
Jeg vil gerne have besked før/inden du rejser.

As a conjunction after a negative main clause = **førend**:

Hans had hardly got home before the telephone rang.
Hans var næppe kommet hjem førend telefonen ringede.

As an adverb = 'earlier', 'previously' = **før**:

Two days before we had met her in town.
To dage før havde vi truffet hende i byen.

As a preposition = **før/inden**:

That was before my time!
Det var før min tid!

Before long spring will be here.
Inden længe bliver det forår.

5 'Both'

As a conjunction ('both A and B') = **både ... og**:

Both Kitty and Jean are foreigners.
Både Kitty og Jean er udlændinge.

As a pronoun ('both Xs') = **begge (to)**:

 They both studied Faroese.
De studerede begge (to) færøsk.

6 'But'

As a conjunction = **men**:

He worked hard but he didn't earn much.
Han arbejdede hårdt, men han tjente ikke meget.

As a preposition (= 'except') = **undtagen/uden**:

All the students but one have passed.
Alle de studerende undtagen én har bestået.

No one but my wife knows.
Ingen uden min kone ved det.

7 'If'

As a general subordinator (= 'whether' = **om**):

I asked her if she would like to dance.
Jeg spurgte hende om hun ønskede at danse.

As a conjunction introducing a conditional clause = **hvis**:

If you don't do your homework then your parents will be angry.
Hvis du ikke læser dine lektier, bliver dine forældre vrede.

8 'That'

As a subordinating conjunction = **at**:

They say (that) they haven't got the time.
De siger (at) de ikke har tid.

As a relative pronoun (= 'which', 'whom') when object = **som**:

He dropped the bottle that he had just bought.
Han tabte flasken som han lige havde købt.

As a relative pronoun (= 'which', 'whom') when subject = either **der** or
som:

There are eleven countries that have applied for membership of the
   EU.
Der er elleve lande der/som har søgt om medlemskab af EU.

In cleft sentences (see **158**) = either **der/som** or **at**:
der/som is used when the correlative is a non-adverbial noun phrase:

It was a dictionary (that) Niels sent me last week.
Det var en ordbog (som) Niels sendte mig i sidste uge.

at is used when the correlative is an adverbial of time or place:

It was in 1985 (that) we graduated.
Det var i 1985 (at) vi tog vores eksamen.

It was in Odense (that) he learnt to speak Danish.
Det var i Odense (at) han lærte at tale dansk.

In the expression 'now that' = **nu da**:

Now that the weather is warmer we can bathe in the lake.
Nu da vejret er blevet varmere, kan vi bade i søen.

As a demonstrative (see **74**):

That girl is really pretty!
Den pige er virkelig smuk!

11 WORD ORDER AND CLAUSE STRUCTURE

137 WORD CLASSES AND CLAUSE ELEMENTS

Elsewhere in this book we examine word classes (or parts of speech), i.e. words grouped according to their form or meaning, e.g. nouns, verbs, etc. In this section of the book we examine clause elements, i.e. words and groups of words and their function and position within the clause. These two approaches are illustrated by the following main clause example:

	Vi	**har**	**ikke**	**set**	**Peter**	**i aften.**
	(We	have	not	seen	Peter	this evening.)
Word class	pronoun	verb	adverb	verb	noun	preposition + noun
Clause element	subject	finite verb	clausal adverbial	non-finite verb	object	other adverbial

Several clause elements (i.e. any word or group of words) can be moved to the beginning of a clause (main clause statement):

I aften har vi ikke set Peter.   This evening we haven't . . .
Peter har vi ikke set i aften.   Peter we haven't . . .

138 CLAUSE TYPES

Most clauses possess both a subject (see **142**) and a finite verb (see **143**).

1 In describing clauses we often use the terms **FV1**-clause and **FV2**-clause:

In **FV1**-clauses the finite verb comes first in the clause.
In **FV2**-clauses the finite verb comes second, after some other element.

2 The five sentence types and the relative positions of the subject, finite verb and other elements in Danish are shown in the table below. Under the *Word order* column, the designation *straight* = subject – finite verb, and the designation *inverted* = finite verb – subject.

Position				
1	*2*	*3*	*4 →*	*Word order*
STATEMENT				
Subject	*Finite verb*	–	*etc.*	*FV2, straight*
Han	**rejser**	–	**hjem i dag.**	
(He is going home today.)				
Non-subject	*Finite verb*	*Subject*	*etc.*	*FV2, inverted*
I dag	**rejser**	**han**	**hjem.**	
(Today he is going home.)				
YES/NO QUESTION				
–	*Finite verb*	*Subject*	*etc.*	*FV1, inverted*
–	**Rejser**	**han**	**hjem i dag?**	
(Is he going home today?)				
–	**Skal**	**han**	**ikke rejse hjem idag?**	
(Isn't he going home today?)				
HV- QUESTION				
hv- word	*Finite verb*	*Subject*	*etc.*	*FV2, inverted*
Hvorfor	**rejser**	**han**	**hjem i dag?**	
(Why is he going home today?)				
hv- word/Subj.	*Finite verb*	–	*etc.*	*FV2, straight*
Hvem	**rejser**	–	**hjem i dag?**	
(Who is going home today?)				
COMMAND				
–	*Finite verb*	–	*etc.*	*FV1, no subject*
–	**Rejs**	–	**hjem!**	
(Go home!)				
WISH				
–	*Finite verb*	*Subject*	*etc.*	*FV1, inverted*
–	**Måtte**	**du**	**dog snart blive rask!**	
(May you get well soon!)				

Notes:

1 **hv-** questions are so called because they begin with an interrogative pronoun/adverb or **hv-** word (see **77**).

2 Yes/no questions are so called because the answer to them is 'yes' or 'no'.

3 Notice the difference in structure between **hv-** questions (FV2) and yes/no questions (FV1).

139 MAIN CLAUSE STRUCTURE

Many main clauses possess other elements not detailed in **138** above. These are included in the schema below, which may be used to explain and analyse most main clauses in Danish. Note the symbols **F v n a V N A** which will be used from now on for each of the seven positions.

1 Front position	2 Finite verb	3 (Subject)	4 Clausal adverbial	5 Non-finite verb	6 Object/ complement/ real subject	7 Other adverbial
F	**v**	**n**	**a**	**V**	**N**	**A**

Sentence type:
STATEMENT

Han	**rejser**	–	–	–	–	**hjem i dag.**
(He is going home today.)						
I morges	**havde**	**han**	**endnu ikke**	**pakket**	**sin kuffert.**	
(This morning he still hadn't packed his suitcase.)						
Sin kuffert	**havde**	**han**	**endnu ikke**	**pakket**	–	**i morges.**
Så	**blev**	**de**	**naturligvis**	–	**vrede.**	
(Then of course they got angry.)						
Der	**sidder**	–	–	–	**to patienter**	**uden for**
(Two patients are sitting outside his office.)						**hans kontor.**

YES/NO QUESTION

–	**Flytter**	**de**	–	–	–	**til Odense?**
(Are they moving to Odense?)						
–	**Vil**	**de**	**ikke**	**flytte**	–	**til Odense?**
(Don't they want to move to Odense?)						
–	**Har**	**du**	**aldrig**	**villet møde**	**hende**	**før?**
(Have you never wanted to meet her before?)						
–	**Gav**	**du**	–	–	**ham pengene?**	
(Did you give him the money?)						

HV- QUESTION

Hvem	**kommer**	–	–	–	–	**her i aften?**
(Who is coming here tonight?)						
Hvem	**gav**	**du**	–	–	**pengene**	**til?**
(Who did you give the money to?)						
Hvornår	**ønsker**	**de**	–	**at rejse**	–	**til Norge?**
(When do they want to go to Norway?)						

COMMAND

–	**Ring**	–	**altid**	–	–	**før kl. tolv!**
(Always ring before twelve o'clock!)						
–	**Kom!**					
(Come!)						

WISH

–	**Måtte**	**der**	**aldrig**	**ske**	**ham noget!**	
(May nothing ever happen to him!)						
Længe	**leve**	**kongen!**				
(Long live the king!)						

Notice that:

1 Main clauses always have a finite verb and usually a subject.
2 All positions except that occupied by the finite verb (v) may be left vacant.
3 The subject usually occupies positions 1 (F) or 3 (n).
4 The front position (F) is always occupied in statements and **hv-** questions, but is vacant in yes/no questions.
5 Only one clause element can usually occupy the front position (F) at any time.
6 There may be more than one clausal adverbial (a), non-finite verb (V), object, complement (N) or other adverbial (A).

140 LINK POSITION

The link position (**k**) is an additional position necessary before the front position (**F**) in order to accommodate conjunctions:

k	F	v	n	a	V	N	A
Han kommer,	**men**	**han**	**bliver** –	**ikke**	–	–	**længe.**

(He is coming, but he won't stay long.)

	F	v	n	a	V	N	A
Venter du,	**eller**	–	**går**	**du**	–	–	–	**nu?**

(Are you waiting or are you going now?)

141 EXTRA POSITIONS

The extra positions (**X₁, X₂**) are additional positions necessary both before the **F**-position and after the **A**-position to accommodate elements of various kinds outside the clause. These elements often duplicate elements within the clause proper.

	X_1	F	v	n	a	V	N	A	X_2
1	**Tom,**	**han**	**er**	–	**jo**	–	**syg**	**i dag.**	
2	**Paris,**	**det**	**er**	–	**vel nok**	–	**en dejlig by!**		
3	**I Esbjerg,**	**der**	**vil**	**jeg**	**gerne**	**bo.**			
4	**Da vi så kom hjem,**	**lavede**	**vi**	–		–	**en kop kaffe.**		
5		**Det**	**er**	–	**ikke**	–	**sandt**	–	**at tiden læger alle sår.**
6		**Det**	**er**	–	–	–	**sjovt**	–	**at spille tennis.**

Translations: 1 Tom, he's ill today. 2 Paris, that's really a lovely city! 3 In Esbjerg, I would like to live there. 4 When we got home, (then) we made a cup of coffee. 5 It's not true that time heals all wounds. 6 It's fun playing tennis.

If there is also a link position (**k**), the order is:

k	X₁	F, etc.
men	**Svend,**	**han er morsom ...**

(but Svend, he's amusing ...)

142   REAL SUBJECT AND FORMAL SUBJECT

The subject may be:

- a noun (phrase):   **Drengen elsker rejer.**   The boy loves prawns.
  Karen står på ski.   Karen is skiing.
  Den grimme ælling   The ugly duckling did not
  kom ikke hjem igen.   come home again.
- a pronoun: **Han skriver et brev.**   He's writing a letter.
- an adjective: **Rødt er da smukt.**   Red is beautiful, isn't it?
- an infinitive (phrase):   **At lyve er slemt.**   Lying is bad.
  At flyve til Billund   Flying to Billund
  er meget billigt.   is very cheap.
- a subordinate clause: **At vi tabte kampen**   That we lost the match is
  er forståeligt.   understandable.

The formal subject (FS) **der** must be inserted when there is a postponed or real subject (RS) that is a noun (phrase):

Der (FS) **sidder en politibetjent** (RS) **i dagligstuen.**
There's a policeman sitting in the living room.
(Cf. **En politibetjent sidder i dagligstuen.**)

If the real subject is an infinitive (phrase), then the formal subject used is **det**:

Det (FS) **er svært at lære dansk** (RS).
It's difficult to learn Danish.

Similarly, formal subjects may be used in questions:

Sidder der en politibetjent ... ?   Er det svært at lære dansk?

143   FINITE VERB

The finite verb is the verb which carries the tense, i.e. which indicates present or past time. The finite forms are, therefore, the simple present and past, and the imperative and subjunctive forms.

Han *løber* hurtigt.	He runs fast.
Han *løb* hurtigt.	He ran fast.
Løb hurtigere!	Run faster!
Formanden længe *leve*!	Three cheers for the chairman!

In two-verb constructions the finite verb is often an auxiliary verb:

Han *har* læst tre romaner i dag.	He has read three novels today.
Han *kan* læse meget hurtigt.	He can read very quickly.

144   NON-FINITE VERB

Non-finite verb forms usually occur only together with a finite verb (**143**). The non-finite forms are the infinitive, present participle and past participle.

Han kan *løbe* hurtigt.	He can run fast.
Han kom *løbende* ned ad gaden.	He came running down the street.
Han har *løbet* hele vejen.	He has run the whole way.

145   CLAUSAL ADVERBIAL

1 The clausal adverbial usually modifies the sense of the clause as a whole. It is often a simple adverb (see also **107**, **151**):

F	v	n	a	etc.	
Vi	**rejser**	–	**aldrig**	**til Danmark om sommeren.**	never
			altid		always
			gerne		willingly
			ikke		not
			jo		of course
			ofte		often

Cf. the comparable word order in the English main clause:

     (a)   **(v)**

We **never** go to Denmark in the summer.

2 Notice the relative order when there are several clausal adverbials:

(a) Short modal adverbs:	**da, jo, nok, nu, vel**
(b) Short pronominal and conjunctional adverbs:	**altså, derfor, dog**
(c) Longer modal adverbs:	**egentlig, muligvis**
(d) Negations:	**aldrig, ikke**

De har nu (1) **altså** (2) **egentlig** (3) **aldrig** (4) **været i København.**
(So in fact they have never been to Copenhagen, you know.
Lit. They have you know so in fact never been in Copenhagen.)

146 OTHER ADVERBIALS

Other adverbials comprise expressions of manner, place, time, condition,
cause, etc. They are sometimes called MPT-adverbials for this reason, and
often consist of a prepositional phrase or of a subordinate clause:

Vi rejser *med toget.* **Vi rejser** *til Århus.* **Vi rejser** *på torsdag.*
      A-manner   *A-place*   *A-time*
(We're going by train . . . to Århus . . . on Thursday.)

Vi kommer *hvis vi får tid.*   **Vi går nu** *fordi vi har travlt.*
      A-condition   *A-cause*
(We'll come if we have time.)   (We'll go now because we're in a hurry.)

Notice that the relative order of other adverbials is usually (but not always):

Vi rejser med toget (manner) **til Århus** (place) **på torsdag** (time)
hvis vi får tid (condition).

Some simple adverbs also function as other adverbials: **vi gik bort/ned/ud**.
These usually come at the end of the clause. The stressed verb particle also
occupies the final adverbial (**A**) position. See also compound verbs, **106**.

1	2	3	4	5	6	7
F	*v*	*n*	*a*	*V*	*N*	*A*
Jeg	**skal**	–	**jo**	**klæde**	**børnene**	**'på.**

(I have to dress the children, you know.)

Vi	**måtte**	–	–	**skrive**	**det hele**	**'ned.**

(We had to write it all down.)

147 OBJECTS AND COMPLEMENTS

Transitive verbs (**103**) take a direct object:

Niels spiser en kage.   Niels is eating a cake.

Intransitive verbs (**103**) take no object:

Niels sidder i sofaen.   Niels is sitting on the sofa.

The direct object (DO) – which goes in the object (**N**) position – may
comprise:

- a noun (phrase):   **Hun har stjålet** *hans bil.*
                            She has stolen his car.

- a pronoun: **Anna har hjulpet _ham_.**
                                    Anna has helped him.

- a subordinate clause: **Jeg ved _at han er der_.**
                                    I know he's there.

For pronouns see also light elements, **150.**

Ditransitive verbs take both a direct and an indirect object (see **103**). The indirect object (IO) is usually a person or thing for whose sake an action is undertaken:

Jeg gav	**Jens**	**min bog.**
	IO	DO

I gave Jens my book.

Jeg gav	**min bog**	**til Jens.**
	DO	IO

I gave my book to Jens.

Notice that the order of the objects is usually as in English, i.e. a preposition-less object precedes an object with a preposition:

Han lånte	**bogen**	**til Niels.**
	– prep	+ prep

(He lent the book to Niels.)

If neither object has a preposition, the indirect object precedes the direct object:

Han lånte	**Niels**	**bogen.**
	IO	DO

(He lent Niels the book.)

The predicative complement occupies the same position as the object (**N**), and is found in sentences with copula verbs like: **blive, gøre ... til ...,** **hedde, kaldes, se ... ud, synes, virke, være.** The complement agrees with the subject or object.

Ole og Marie er studerende.   (= Subject complement)
Ole and Marie are students.

De virker meget intelligente.
They seem very intelligent.

When there is an object, the complement follows it and relates to it:

Det gjorde ham glad.   (= Object complement)
That made him happy.

De kaldte deres hund Bob.
They called their dog Bob.

148   PASSIVE AGENT

See passive, **105**. The passive agent usually occupies the final (other) adverbial position (**A**), and will normally come immediately before any other adverbial expression:

F	v	n	a	V	N	A
De gamle	**bør**	–	**bestemt**	**hjælpes**	–	**af kommunen.**

(Old people should certainly be helped by the local authority.)

Peter	**blev**	–	–	**klippet**	–	**af sin kone i går.**

(Peter had his hair cut by his wife yesterday.)

149   TOPICALISATION

1 The subject most frequently occupies the front position (**F**), but it may be replaced by moving to the front almost any other clause element. This is often done when one wishes to emphasise a particular clause element, or for stylistic reasons, and is known as topicalisation. When the subject is not in the **F**-position, it follows the finite verb (**n**-position).

	F	v	n	a	V	N	A
Basic clause:	**Han**	**vil**	–	**alligevel**	**sælge**	**huset**	**i år.**

(He'll sell the house this year, anyway.)

	F	v	n	a	V	N	A
1 (**A** to **F**):	**I år**	**vil**	**han**	**alligevel**	**sælge**	**huset.**	←
2 (**N** to **F**):	**Huset**	**vil**	**han**	**alligevel**	**sælge**	←	**i år.**
3 (**a** to **F**):	**Alligevel**	**vil**	**han**	←	**sælge**	**huset**	**i år.**

When the non-finite verb is moved to **F**, the elements governed by it will normally also be moved with it:

	F	v	n	a	V	N	A
4 (**V** + **N** to **F**):	**Sælge huset**	**vil**	**han**	**alligevel**	←	←	**i år.**
5 (**V** + **N** + **A** to **F**):	**Sælge huset i år**	**vil**	**han**	**alligevel.**	←	←	←

Topicalisation of adverbials which usually occupy the other adverbial position (**A**), especially of time and place (including **her**, **der**), is by far the most frequent type:

Vi tog til Møn i foråret.   → **I foråret tog vi til Møn.**
We went to Møn last spring.   → Last spring we went to Møn.

Hans drak Guinness i Dublin.   → **I Dublin drak Hans Guinness.**
Hans drank Guinness in Dublin.   → In Dublin Hans drank Guinness.

Hun har aldrig været *her/der.* → *Her/Der* **har hun aldrig været.**
She has never been *here/there.*   She has never been *here/there.*

In the **F**-position it is common to find a subordinate clause which would otherwise be in the other adverbial position:

Vi tog til Møn da vi kom hjem fra Frankrig.
We went to Møn when we got back from France.

→ **Da vi kom hjem fra Frankrig, tog vi til Møn.**
When we got back from France we went to Møn.

Proper nouns and object pronouns are also commonly topicalised:

Ulla har vi ikke set længe.   **Hende har vi ikke set længe.**
We haven't seen Ulla for a long time.   We haven't seen her for a long time.

It is possible to topicalise direct speech:

'Fy dog!' sagde han.   'Shame on you!' he said.

The subject complement may also occasionally be topicalised:

Høflig har han aldrig været!
He's never been polite!

2 Natural topics:
Most natural topics are unstressed and represent familiar information or are used to link sentences together:

Vi trængte til en ferie, så i september kørte vi til Jylland. Der traf vi nogle gamle venner. De ejer en stor villa. Den har ti værelser. Vi boede der i 14 dage. Så måtte vi desværre vende hjem igen.
We needed a holiday, so in September we drove to Jutland. There we met some old friends. They own a large house. It has ten rooms. We stayed there for a fortnight. Then unfortunately we had to come home again.

3 Emphatic topics:
These are rarer and often represent new information. The following emphatic topics are either stylistically marked or used for contrast:

Rart var det nu ikke!   But it wasn't very nice!
En avis købte vi også.   A newspaper we bought too.
Det kan jeg ikke tro!   That I cannot believe!
Løbe efter piger kan han, men   Run after girls, that he can do,
studere vil han ikke.   but study he will not.

150   LIGHT ELEMENTS

'Light' elements are short, unstressed clause elements, e.g. object pronouns and reflexive pronouns. In clauses without a non-finite verb (i.e. the V-position is empty), they always move leftwards into the subject position (**n**) after the finite verb. An indirect object (IO) with no preposition will nevertheless always precede the direct object (DO).

F	v	n	a	V	N	A
Jeg	**kender**	**ham**	**ikke.**			
		(light DO)				
Jeg	**har**	–	**aldrig**	**kendt**	**ham.**	
Jeg	**kender**	–	**ikke**		*ham.*	
					(stressed DO)	
Hun	**gav**	**mig**	**ikke**	–	**bogen.**	
		(light DO)				
Hun	**har**	–	–	**givet**	**mig**	
					bogen.	
					(IO + DO)	
Hun	**gav**	**mig den**	**ikke.**			
		(light IO + DO)				
Hun	**gav**	–	**ikke**	–	*mig* **den.**	
					(stressed IO)	
Henrik	**vasker**	**sig**	**ikke.**			
Henrik	**har**	–	**ikke**	**vasket**	**sig**	**i dag.**

Translations: I don't know him./I have never known him./I don't know *him.*   She didn't give me the book./She has given me the book./She didn't give me it./She didn't give *me* it. Henrik doesn't wash./Henrik hasn't washed today.

Similarly, the adverbs **her** 'here' and **der** 'there' move leftwards to occupy the **n**-position when they are unstressed and the **V**-position is vacant:

> **Hun var her/der ikke.** (= unstressed)
> **Hun var ikke *her/der*.** (= stressed)

But:

> **Hun har ikke været her/der.**   She has not been here/there.

151   POSITION OF **IKKE** AND NEGATIVE ELEMENTS

The position of **ikke** 'not' and other negative adverbials, e.g. **aldrig** 'never', etc., can vary. When they negate the entire clause they occupy the clausal adverbial **a**-position immediately after the finite verb or subject (see **139ff**):

Peter kommer ikke i dag. I dag kommer Peter ikke. I dag er Peter ikke kommet. Peter vil aldrig gøre det.
Peter isn't coming today. Today Peter isn't coming. Today Peter hasn't come. Peter will never do it.

Occasionally, for contrast, the negative may come between the finite verb and the subject in inverted statements:

I dag kommer ikke kun *Peter*, men også hans familie.
Today it's not only *Peter* who is coming but also his family.

Pronominal or noun phrase objects containing a negation are also attracted to the **a**-position:

Jeg havde ikke gjort noget.
I hadn't done anything.

But:

Jeg havde ingenting gjort.

Katten har ikke fået noget mad i dag.
The cat hasn't had any food today.

But:

Katten har ingen mad fået i dag.

Preben har ikke set noget.
Preben hasn't seen anything.

But:

Preben har intet set.

For the position of negative elements in subordinate clauses, see **156**.

152   PASSIVE TRANSFORMATION

By transforming the active verb into a passive form, some of the other elements change position within the clause (see **105**):

Active verb   **Andersen** (= subject) **ejer hele huset** (= object).
Andersen owns the whole house.

Passive verb   **Hele huset** (= subject) **ejes af Andersen** (= Prep.Comp.).
The whole house is owned by Andersen.

Passive transformation can be used in both main or subordinate clauses. For the position of elements in the passive sentence, see **148**.

153   EXISTENTIAL SENTENCES

If we do not wish to introduce a subject at the beginning of a clause, we can postpone it (i.e. move it rightwards), but must then fill the front position (**F**) with a formal subject (place-holder subject); the postponed subject is known as the real subject (cf. **142**):

> **En betjent sidder inde i køkkenet.** → **Der sidder en betjent inde i**
> **køkkenet.**
>
> Subject   Formal   Real
>   subject   subject
> A policeman is sitting in the kitchen. There's a policeman sitting in
>   the kitchen.

> **At holde op med at ryge er svært.** → **Det er svært at holde op med**
> **at ryge.**
>
> Subject   FS   RS
> Stopping smoking is hard.   It's hard to stop smoking.

(1) Type 1: When the real subject is an indefinite noun phrase (like **en betjent**), then it occupies the **N**-position:

F	v	n	a	V	N	A
Der	findes	–	–	–	**ingen bjerge**	**i Danmark.**
Der	sidder	–	ofte	–	**en betjent**	**inde i køkkenet.**
–	Sidder	der	ofte	–	**en betjent**	**inde i køkkenet?**

Translations: There are no mountains in Denmark.   There's often a policeman sitting in the kitchen.   Is there often a policeman sitting in the kitchen?

The verb in Danish existential sentences is always intransitive, and usually expresses:

- existence: **findes**
- non-existence: **mangle, savne**
- location: **ligge, sidde, stå, være**
- motion: **gå, komme**

In English the only corresponding constructions are: 'there is (are) -ing'. Note that in this case the formal subject is **der** = 'there'.

(2) Type 2: When the real subject is an infinitive phrase (like **at holde op med at ryge**), then it occupies the **X₂** position (see also **141f**, **156**):

F	v	n	a	V	N	A	X₂
Det	er	–	–	–	**dejligt**	–	**at svømme.**
Det	er	–	altid	–	**svært**	–	**at være en** **god taber.**

Translations: It's lovely to swim. It's always hard to be a good loser.

Note that in this case the formal subject is **det** = 'it'.

154   SUBORDINATE CLAUSE AS AN ELEMENT IN THE MAIN CLAUSE

1 Subordinate clauses usually constitute the subject, object or other adverbial in a main clause sentence. As such they may occupy several different positions:

F	v	n	a	V	N	A	X₂

Subject clause:

| *At du er rask,* | **glæder** | **mig** | – | – | – | **meget.** | |
| **Det** | **glæder** | **mig** | – | – | – | **meget** | *at du er rask.* |

Object clause:

| **Han** | | **sagde** | – | **ikke** | – | – | **i går** | *at han skal giftes på lørdag.* |

| *At han skal giftes på lørdag* | **sagde** | **han** | **ikke** | – | – | **i går.** | |

Adverbial clause:

| **Vi** | | **går** | – | – | – | – | *når han kommer.* |
| *Når han kommer,* | **går** | **vi.** | | | | | |

Translations: That you are well makes me very glad. I am very glad that you are well.   He didn't say yesterday that he was getting married on Saturday.   That he was getting married on Saturday he did not say yesterday.   We will go when he comes. When he comes we will go.

Notice that:

- Subject and object clauses occupy the **F** or **X₂** positions.
- Most adverbial clauses (time, condition, cause) occupy the **F** or **A** positions.
- Some adverbial clauses (intention, result) can only occupy the **A** position:

F	v	n	a	V	N	A
Vi	**må**	–	–	**støtte**	**ham**	*for at han ikke skal falde.*
Jeg	**blev**	–	–	–	**så vred**	*at jeg straks gik hjem.*

Translations: We have to support him so that he doesn't fall. I got so angry that I went home right away.

2 A relative clause usually functions as an attribute to the correlative, usually a noun:

Han kiggede på de piger *som sad på græsset.*
He looked at the girls who were sitting on the grass.

Den film (som) *vi så i går,* **var fantastisk.**
The film we saw yesterday was fantastic.

Den dreng *der var uartig,* **fik ikke lov at komme med til festen.**
The boy who was naughty was not allowed to go to the party.

155   MAIN CLAUSE STRUCTURE – AN EXTENDED POSITIONAL SCHEMA WITH EXAMPLES

	k	X_1	1 F	2 v	3 n	4 a	5 V	6 N	7 A	X_2
1			Han	havde	–	ikke	pakket	kufferten	i morges.	
2			I morges	havde	han	ikke	pakket	kufferten.		
3			Vi	giver	–	–	–	Ole en gave	i aften.	
4			Siden	blev	de	desværre	–	syge.		
5			Det	gjorde	–	–	–	ham glad.		
6			Der	er	–	allerede	kommet	to betjente.		
7	Og –		det	er	–	da	–	så sjovt	–	at spille tennis.
8			Henrik	ville	–	jo altid	kysse	os,	–	Marie og mig.
9	men Niels,		han	er	–	nu ikke	–	så tosset.		
10			Bilen	blev	–	–	repareret	–	i går.	
11			Jeg	blev	–	–	hentet	–	af Lise på banegården i går.	
12			Katten	er	–	–	løbet	–	bort.	
13			Jeg	skal	–	jo	klæde	børnene	på.	
14			Hun	kan	–	–	læse	–	meget hurtigt.	
15			I går	kedede	han	ikke.				
				sig						
16			De	har	–	aldrig	giftet	sig.		
17			Vi	kender	ham	ikke.				
18			Sælge huset	vil	han	alligevel ikke	–	–	i år.	
19				Kom!						

Translations: 1 He had not packed the case this morning. 2 This morning he had not packed his case. 3 We are giving Ole a present this evening. 4 Then unfortunately they became ill. 5 It made him happy. 6 Two policemen have already come. 7 And it's such fun of course playing tennis. 8 Henrik always wanted to kiss us, you know, Marie and me. 9 But Niels, he's not that stupid, as a matter of fact. 10 The car was

repaired yesterday.   11 I was met by Lise at the railway station yesterday.
12 The cat has run away.   13 I have to dress the children, you know.
14 She can read very quickly.   15 Yesterday he wasn't bored.   16 They
have never got married.   17 We don't know him.   18 He won't sell the
house this year, anyway.   19 Come!

KEY to the above schema: *For details*
                                                                   see
                                                                   paragraph:

k = link position   **140**
    (conjunction)
X₁ = extra position   – duplicates elements in the clause **141**
F = front position   – any clause element except the   **139, 153,**
                                  finite verb. Normally there is   **154**
                                  only one element in this position.
v = finite verb   – present or past tense or   **143**
                                  imperative
n = nominals   – subject (if not in **F**), reflexive **139, 150**
                                  pronoun, unstressed pronominal
                                  object ('light') elements
a = clausal adverb(ial)   – short modal adverb, short   **145, 151**
                                  conjunctional/pronominal adverb,
                                  longer modal adverb, negation
V = non-finite verb   – infinitive, present or past   **144**
                                  participle
N = nominals   – real subject, subject complement, **147, 153,**
                                  indirect object, direct object,   **154**
                                  object complement
A = other adverbial   – verb particle, passive agent,   **146, 148**
                                  manner adverbial, place
                                  adverbial, time adverbial, long
                                  adverbials
X₂ = extra position   – duplicates elements in the   **141, 154**
                                  sentence, subject and object
                                  clauses

156   SUBORDINATE CLAUSE STRUCTURE

Subordinate clauses (which, as we have seen above, may simply be considered as elements in main clauses) also possess an internal structure of
their own which differs from that of main clauses as follows:

Context	1 Conjunc- tion	2 Subj.	3 Clausal adverbial	4 Finite verb	5 Non- finite verb	6 Object/ comp.	7 Other adverbial
	k	**n**	**a**	**v**	**V**	**N**	**A**
Vi rejser	**når**	**han**	–	**kommer.**			
Vi spurgte	**om**	**han**	–	**havde**	**pakket**	**kufferten.**	
–	**Eftersom**	**de**	**ikke**	**havde**	**sagt**	**et ord,**	– vidste vi intet.
Hun sagde	**(at)**	**det**	**ikke**	**var**	–	**morsomt**	**længere.**
Hvis vi er stille,	**og hvis**	**vi**	**ikke**	**er**	–	**uartige,**	– **må vi se** **TV i** **aften.**

Translations: We will leave when he comes.   We asked whether he had packed the case.   As they hadn't said a word we knew nothing.   She said it wasn't funny any more.   If we're quiet and we're not naughty, we'll be allowed to watch TV tonight.

Notice the following characteristics of the subordinate clause:

1 There is no **F**-position in the subordinate clause; the order is always: conjunction – subject – clausal adverbial – finite verb, i.e.:

- The clause always begins with a subordinating conjunction or other subordinator, except for certain uses of **at** and **som** (see **75–76, 156.3**).
- The clausal adverbial comes immediately before the finite verb.
- The word order is straight, i.e. the subject comes before the finite verb.

2 The subject position (**n**) is always occupied. If there is both a formal and a real subject, the latter is postponed to the object position (**N**).

3 The conjunction **at** (that) may sometimes be omitted:

Frederik lovede (at) han ikke ville sige noget.
Frederik promised (that) he wouldn't say anything.

Jeg håber (at) jeg snart kan træffe dig igen.
I hope (that) I can meet you again soon.

4 The guidelines and rules concerning main clause word order outlined earlier apply equally to subordinate clauses, with the exception of the following:

(a) 'Light' or unstressed pronouns, whether as direct or indirect objects, and **her** and **der**, do not move leftwards to the **n**-position but remain in the **N**-position:

... selvom han ikke gav mig det.
... although he didn't give me it.

. . . skønt jeg aldrig er der.
. . . even though I'm never there.

(b) There is no initial extra position in subordinate clauses; any other elements will appear at the end of the clause in the same way as in main clauses:

. . . fordi han var enormt beruset, den fyr.
. . . because he was extremely drunk, that chap.

(c) The subject will appear first in most subordinate clauses, i.e. the topicalisation of other elements cannot normally happen (but see **159**).

(d) The **k**-position is used here to indicate a subordinating conjunction; should there also be a coordinating conjunction introducing the subordinate clause, this is placed in the same position immediately preceding the subordinating conjunction, e.g.: . . . , **og fordi** . . . (. . . , and because . . .).

157   INDEPENDENT CLAUSES

An independent clause is a subordinate clause which stands alone as a sentence and does not therefore form part of a larger sentence. It is usually an exclamation or a wish, and has the same structure as other subordinate clauses:

k	**n**	**a**	**v**	**V**	**N**	**A**
Hvis	**du**	**bare**	**vidste**	–	**det hele!**	

(If you only knew everything!)

At	**I**	**ikke**	**bliver**	–	**trætte!**	

(That you don't get tired!)

Clauses beginning with the words **bare**, **blot**, **gid**, **mon** have subordinate clause word order:

Gid hun ikke var så syg!
If only she weren't so ill!

Mon han nogensinde finder sig en kone?
I wonder if he'll ever find a wife.

158   CLEFT SENTENCES

In order to emphasise an element together with the action of the verb, that element (X) may be extracted from the sentence and inserted into the construction:

Det er/var X som/der . . .   It is/was X who/that . . .

The remainder of the original sentence is downgraded and relegated to a subordinate clause added onto the end. Notice that **der** and **som** are used to refer to a non-adverbial noun phrase or pronoun, and **at** (unless omitted) is used to refer to a time or place adverbial:

Cf.   **Klaus sendte mig en bog i sidste uge.**
         Klaus sent me a book last week.

→ **Det var en bog (som) Klaus sendte mig i sidste uge.**
    It was a book that Klaus . . .

→ **Det var Klaus der sendte mig en bog i sidste uge.**
    It was Klaus who . . .

→ **Det var i sidste uge (at) Klaus sendte mig en bog.**
    It was last week that Klaus . . .

The cleft sentence is also very common in questions:

Var det oppositionslederen der kritiserede regeringen?
Was it the leader of the opposition who criticised the government?
(Cf. **Kritiserede oppositionslederen regeringen?**)

Er det dig der bestemmer her?
Is it you who decides here?

Er det øl han drikker?
Is it beer he drinks?

159   THREE TYPES OF SUBORDINATE CLAUSE WITH MAIN CLAUSE STRUCTURE

These are all exceptions, in different ways, to **156** above, in that the subordinate clause forms part of a sentence (cf. **154**) but has a word order structure that can be the same as that of the main clause (see **139, 155**).

1 **At-** clauses with a 'topic':
Subordinate clauses which are reported speech usually have subordinate clause word order, yet in spoken and informal written language it is increasingly common for an element to follow the conjunction as a kind of topic. When a non-subject comes immediately after the conjunction **at**, the finite verb and subject are inverted (i.e. main clause word order):

Frederik sagde, at *i går* var hele familien i Tivoli.
Frederik said that yesterday the whole family went to Tivoli.

2 **At-** clauses with finite verb – clausal adverb order:
In some cases the clausal adverbial adopts the same position as in the main clause, i.e. after the finite verb, rather than its usual subordinate clause position before the finite verb:

Frederik sagde, at han *skulle ikke* på arbejde i dag.
Frederik said that he wasn't going to work today.

This is only found in spoken Danish and should never be written. Write:

Frederik sagde, at han *ikke skulle* på arbejde i dag.

An explanation for this order is that the **at-** clause is regarded as a statement in direct speech, i.e. as a main clause, cf.:

Frederik sagde: 'Jeg *skal ikke* på arbejde i dag.'
Frederik said: 'I'm not going to work today.'

The conjunction **at** functions therefore in almost the same way as a colon.

3 Conditional clauses with yes/no question order:
Conditional clauses are usually introduced by **hvis**:

Hvis du ikke skriver til mor, bliver hun ked af det.
If you don't write to Mother she'll feel sad.

But conditional clauses may have no subordinating conjunction, and rely on inverted word order (finite verb – subject) to indicate condition:

Skriver du ikke til mor, bliver hun ked af det. (Conditional)
Cf. **Skriver du ikke til mor?** (Yes/no question)

Clauses of this type also occur in English:

Had I known you were arriving, I would have waited.
Were you to agree to this, it would be disastrous.

160 MAJOR WORD ORDER AND CLAUSE STRUCTURE PROBLEMS – SUMMARY

A number of aspects of word order are similar in Danish and English. This summary concentrates only on some of the major differences.

Key: **S**	= subject	
O	= object	
V	= finite verb	
Advl	= clausal adverbial	
T	= clause element (non-subject) which may come first in the clause	

1 Main clause – inversion (**138**, **149**, **155**)

Danish:	*English:*	
S–V–T	S–V–T	
Han sover nu.	He is asleep now.	In Danish non-subjects often come first in the
		main clause, and this
T–V–S	T–S–V	causes inversion of subject
Nu sover han.	Now he is asleep.	and finite verb.
		In English the order is always subject-verb.

2 Main clause – adverb(ial)s (e.g. **ikke**, **aldrig**) (**145**, **151**, **155**)

S–V–Advl	S–Advl–V	
De leger aldrig.	They never play.	In main clauses in Danish the clausal adverbial (adverb) usually comes immediately after the finite verb. In English it usually comes immediately before the finite verb.

3 Subordinate clause – adverb(ial)s (e.g. **ikke**, **aldrig**) (**156**, **159**)

S-Advl-V	S-V-Advl	
De sagde at de ikke havde skrevet.	They said that they had not written.	In subordinate clauses in Danish the clausal adverbial (adverb) always
	S-Advl-V	comes immediately before
De ved at jeg aldrig drikker.	They know that I never drink.	the finite verb. In English the order varies.

Remember: subject – **ikke** – verb in Danish.

4 Objects, etc., with and without stress (**150**)

S-V-Advl-O	S-V-Advl-O	
Jeg kender ikke *ham*.	I don't know *him*.	When object pronouns lose their stress in Danish they
S-V-O-Advl		move left in the sentence.
Jeg kender ham ikke.	I don't know him.	In English stress is used.

12 WORD FORMATION

161 INTRODUCTION

The vocabulary of Danish is constantly being altered by five main processes:

1 Borrowing from other languages:

English 'a strike'	→ **en strejke**	strike

2 Compounding of existing stems:

en cykel + **en hjelm**	→ **en cykelhjelm**	cycle helmet

3 Affixation:

u- + **ven**	→ **uven** (*lit.* 'un-friend')	enemy

4 Abbreviation:

præventiv-pille	→ **p-pille**	contraceptive pill

5 Change of form, meaning or word class:

et veto (noun)	→ **at vetoe** (verb)	

Borrowing from other languages normally involves the eventual assimilation of a loanword into the Danish system of orthography, pronunciation and inflexion.

162 COMPOUNDING

1 The first element of a compound may be a noun, adjective, verb, pronoun, numeral, adverb, preposition or word group, while the second element is usually a noun, adjective or verb:

Noun + noun:	**sommer|ferie**	(summer holiday)
Noun + verb:	**kæde|ryge**	(chain smoke)
Noun + adjective:	**kul|sort**	(black as coal)
Verb + noun:	**skrive|bord**	(writing desk)
Verb + adjective:	**køre|klar**	(ready to drive away)
Verb + verb:	**øs|regne**	(rain cats and dogs)

For separable and inseparable compound verbs see **106**.

2 Compound nouns may be formed by three main methods:

- noun + noun   **pige|skole**   (girls' school)
- noun + link **-e-** + noun   **jul|e|dag**   (Christmas Day)
- noun + link **-s-** + noun   **forsikring|s|præmie**   (insurance premium)

Notice that the second element in compounds determines the gender and inflexion of the compound:

en **skole** + *et* **køkken** → *et* **skole|køkken**, a school kitchen

Whether or not **-s-** is used as a link between nouns depends to some extent on the form of the elements (first element = FE in what follows).
An **s-** link is usual in nouns that:

- have an FE ending in **-dom, -else, -hed, -(n)ing, -sel, -skab**:

    kristendom|s|undervisning, ledelse|s|struktur, sundhed|s|farlig, landing|s|bane, fødsel|s|kontrol, redskab|s|skur

- have an FE ending in one of the borrowed Romance suffixes **-ion, -tion, -tet, -um**:

    opinion|s|måling, navigation|s|skole, pietet|s|følelse, petroleum|s|kamin

- have an FE which is itself a compound:

    rød|vin|s|glas   cf. **vin|glas**
    skrive|bord|s|skuffe   cf. **bord|skuffe**

An **e-** link is found in some compound nouns which derives from either an original genitive (**natt|e|leje**) or a plural (**engl|e|skare**), but it also occurs in the following cases:

- when the FE ends in a consonant and the SE (second element) begins with a consonant:

    ost|e|mad, sogn|e|præst

- when the FE is a word for a living being and ends in the suffix **-ing**:

    viking|e|flåde, yngling|e|alder

3 First element forms:

(a) When they are FE, nouns are usually found in their singular (uninflected) form: **bil|sæde**.

Exceptions: **blomster|bed, børne|have**.

(b) When they are FE, adjectives are found in their basic form: **gråt vejr** → **grå|vejr**.

Exceptions: **nyt|år, små|børn**.

(c) When they are FE, verbs are found in their infinitive form: **skrive|mask-
ine, spille|mand**.

Exceptions: Verb stems occasionally form the FE: **brus|hane, byg|mester**.

163   AFFIXATION

1 Affixation involves adding a prefix to the beginning or a suffix to the end
of a stem. Whilst prefixes do not alter the word class or inflexion of the stem,
suffixes are often employed precisely to form words of a different class:

Prefix

u-	+ **ven**	→ **uven**
negative prefix	*noun*	*noun*
	friend	enemy

Suffix

venlig	+ **-hed**	→ **venlighed**
adjective	*noun suffix*	*noun*
friendly		friendliness

tank	+ **-e**	→ **tanke**
noun	*verb suffix*	*verb*
tank		to fill up the tank

2 The same basic meaning may be expressed by several different prefixes,
e.g. the words **dis**harmoni, **ikke**-vold, **in**tolerant, **non**konformisme and
ulykkelig all have negative prefixes. The same is true of some suffixes:
udvandr**er**, emigr**ant**, inspek**tor** and inspek**tør** all have suffixes meaning 'a
person carrying out a specific task'. Generally speaking, prefixes and
suffixes are much vaguer in meaning than the stems they modify.

3 Productive and non-productive affixes:
Productive affixes are those still being used to form derivatives whose
meaning can be predicted from the form:

   -agtig = like, as in: **friskfyragtig**, sparky, like Jack the Lad
   -bar = possible to, as in: **bærbar**, possible to carry, portable

Non-productive affixes are those no longer used to form derivatives:

   -dom in: **fattigdom, sygdom, ungdom**, etc.

Non-productive affixes may have been borrowed in many loanwords but
have never been used to form any new indigenous derivatives, e.g.: Latin
kon-: **konflikt, konsonant**.

4 Prefixes – the following is a list of some frequent examples.

Group/prefix	Meaning	Examples	Translation
Negative and pejorative			
u-	not, opposite of, bad	**ukonventionel, uven** **uvane**	unconventional, enemy bad habit
il-	not, opposite of	**illegal**	illegal
im-	not, opposite of	**immobil**	immobile
in-	not, opposite of	**intolerant**	intolerant
ir-	not, opposite of	**irrelevant**	irrelevant
non-	not, opposite of	**nonkonformisme**	non-conformity
mis-	abuse bad	**misbruger** **mislyd**	addict dissonance
van-	wrongly bad	**vanskabt** **vanrøgte**	misshapen neglect
Attitude			
ko-	together with	**koordinere**	coordinate
kol-	together with	**kollaboratør**	collaborator
kom-	together with	**kompagnon**	partner
kon-	together with	**kongenial**	congenial
kor-	together with	**korrespondere**	correspond
sam-	together with	**samboer**	partner, cohabitee
sær-	separate from	**særtilfælde**	special circumstance
anti-	against	**antikommunist**	anti-communist
kontra-	against	**kontrarevolution**	counter-revolution
pro-	favourable towards	**provestlig**	pro-western
Location or direction			
eks-	from	**ekskludere**	exclude
trans-	across	**transplantation**	transplantation
Direction (time or place)			
an-	to, towards	**ankomme**	arrive
for-	away from	**fordrive**	expel
und-	away from	**undslippe**	escape
gen-	back, again	**genfinde**	rediscover
re-	back, again	**reetablere**	re-establish
fort-	further	**fortsætte**	continue
videre-	further	**videreuddannelse**	further education
Number			
mono-	one	**monoteist**	monotheist
bi-	two	**bilateral**	bilateral
tve-	two	**tvekamp**	duel
pan-	all	**panamerikansk**	Pan-American
Conversion verb to verb			
an-	transitivising	**råbe**, call	→ **anråbe**, shout/hail
be-	transitivising	**bo**, live	→ **bebo**, inhabit
Conversion adjective to verb			
be-	make into X	**fri**, free	→ **befri**, liberate
for-	make into X	**ny**, new	→ **forny**, renew

5 Suffixes – the following is a list of some frequent examples.

Group/suffix	Deriving from	Meaning			Examples	Translation
NOUN-FORMING						
People						
-ant	V-**ere**	person			**musikant**	musician
-ent	V-**ere**	person			**assistent**	assistant
-at		person			**demokrat**	democrat
-er		person			**snedker**	joiner
-er		agent of an action			**bager**	baker
-er		nationality			**belgier**	Belgian
-iner		person			**filipiner**	Filipino
-ing, -ling, -ning		origin			**islænding**	Icelander
					ætling	descendant
					flygtning	refugee
-iker	N-**ik**	occupation			**politiker**	politician
-ist	V-**e**, N	occupation, hobby			**motionist**	jogger
-ør	V-**ere**	occupation			**inspektør**	inspector
Feminine						
-inde					**værtinde**	hostess
-esse	N				**prinsesse**	princess
-ske	V-**e**, N-**er**				**plejerske**	nurse
-trice	N-**ør**				**direktrice**	(female) director
-øse	N-**ør**, V-**ere**				**massøse**	masseuse
Activity						
-ende	V-**e**				**forehavende**	project
-else	V-**e**	activity			**følelse**	feeling
-(n)ing	V-**e**	activity			**skrivning**	writing
	V-**e**	activity			**udvikling**	development
-sel	V-**e**	activity			**indførsel**	importation
-sion	V-**ere**	**eksplod/ere**	explode	→	**eksplosion**	explosion
-ition	V-**ere**	**kompon/ere**	compose	→	**komposition**	composition
-(a)tion	V-**ere**	**inform/ere**	inform	→	**information**	information
		fung/ere	function	→	**funktion**	function
Zero suffix	V-**e**				**duft**	fragrance
					sult	hunger
Abstractions						
-ance					**elegance**	elegance
-ence					**kompetence**	competence
-ens					**frekvens**	frequency
-dom	N, A				**sygdom**	illness
-else	V-**e**				**fristelse**	temptation
-ende					**velbefindende**	well-being
-hed					**medlidenhed**	compassion
-ing	V-**e**				**afmagring**	slimming
-isme					**socialisme**	socialism
-itet	A				**popularitet**	popularity
-sel	V-**e**				**glemsel**	oblivion
-skab	N, A				**ondskab**	evil

Group/suffix	Deriving from	Meaning	Examples	Translation
ADJECTIVE-FORMING				
From verbs				
-abel	V-**ere**	possible	**diskutabel**	debatable
-ibel	V-**ere**	possible	**disponibel**	disposable
-at	V-**ere**		**separat**	separate
-bar	V-**e**	possible	**vaskbar**	washable
-et	V-**e**		**nystartet**	recently launched
-et	V-**ere**		**indstuderet**	rehearsed
-lig	V-**e**	possible	**læselig**	readable
-ig	V	inclination	**syndig**	sinful
-sk	V, A	inclination	**indbildsk**	conceited
-som	V, A	inclination	**arbejdsom**	hard-working
-(t)iv	V-**ere**	inclination	**demonstrativ**	demonstrative
From nouns				
-agtig	N	characteristic of	**barnagtig**	childish
-ant	N-**ance/-ence**		**elegant**	elegant
-el	N	belonging to	**kulturel**	cultural
-(e)lig	N	belonging to	**kristelig**	Christian
-en	N	which have X	**ulden**	woollen
-ent	N		**intelligent**	intelligent
-et	N	which have X	**enarmet**	one-armed
-ig	N	which have X	**listig**	sly
-(i)sk	N	belonging to	**britisk**	British
			hollandsk	Dutch
-iv	N-**tion/-sion**		**aktiv**	active
-mæssig	N	in accordance with	**kontraktmæssig**	contractual
-ær	N		**litterær**	literary
-øs	N		**nervøs**	nervous
From adjectives				
-agtig	A	like	**blødagtig**	soft
-artet	A	having the property of	**godartet**	benign
VERB-FORMING				
From nouns				
-e/-ere	N	add/provide with	**adressere, farve**	address, colour
	N	remove	**affugte, støvsuge**	dehumidify, hoover
	N	place in	**logere**	lodge
	N	do	**cykle, vaske kritisere**	cycle, wash criticise
	N	be, act as (with prefix)	**vikariere forklare amerikanisere**	stand in explain Americanise
From adjectives				
-e	N, A	make, change into (with prefix) (with prefix)	**varme, tørre bemyndige forbitre**	heat, dry authorise embitter
-ne	A	become X	**gulne, mørkne**	turn yellow, darken

164 ABBREVIATION

Abbreviation involves the loss of a morpheme or part of a morpheme. Abbreviations arise from three different processes.

1 Clipping – reduction at the beginning or end of a word:

	Whole morpheme lost		*Part morpheme lost*	
Initial reduction:	**(bi)cykel**	bicycle	**(frika)delle**	meatball
Final reduction:	**kilo(gram)**	kilogramme	**krimi(nalroman)**	detective novel

2 Blend (or telescope reduction) – the middle of a word is removed:

m(erværdi)oms(ætningsafgift) (= **moms**)   value added tax

3 Acronym – only an initial letter or letters remain after reduction. Acronyms are of three kinds:

(a) Alphabetisms – the initials are pronounced as letters of the alphabet: **LO** ['el'o:], (Danish Trades Union Congress); **bh** ['be:'hå:], bra(ssiere).

(b) Acronyms pronounced as words: **Nato** ['na:to:], **Saab** [sa:b].

(c) Hybrid forms: **p-plads (parkeringsplads)**; car park; **u-båd (undervands-båd)**, submarine.

165 LIST OF COMMON ABBREVIATIONS

What follows is not a full list, but a number of dictionaries of abbreviations are currently available.

adb	**automatisk databehandling**	**art.**	**1 artikel** **2 artium**, e.g. **mag.art.**
adr.	**adresse**	**A/S, a/s**	**aktieselskab**
AF	**arbejdsformidlingen**	**ass.**	**assistent**
afd.	**1 afdeling** **2 afdøde**	**ATP**	**arbejdsmarkedets tillægspension**
afg.	**afgang**	**aug.**	**august**
afs.	**afsender**	**att.**	**attention (til)**
alm.	**almindelig**	**aut.**	**1 automatisk**
a.m.b.a.	**andelsselskab med begrænset ansvar**	**bd.**	**2 autoriseret** **bind**
ang.	**angående**	**bl.a.**	**blandt andet/andre**
ank.	**ankomst**	**C**	**Celsius**
anm.	**1 anmeldelse** **2 anmærkning**	**c.**	**cent**
		ca.	**cirka**
apr.	**april**	**cand.**	**candidatus**
ApS	**anpartsselskab**	**c.c.**	**carbon copy (kopi til)**

cf.	confer (jævnfør)		3 født
civiling.	civilingeniør		4 følgende (side)
d.	1 den	feb.	februar
	2 død	ff.	følgende (sider)
dat.	dateret	fa.	firma(et)
dav.	daværende	fakt.	faktura
d.d.	dags dato	f.eks.	for eksempel
d.e.	det er (det vil sige)	fhv.	forhenværende
dec.	december	fk.	fælleskøn
dir.	1 direkte	f.Kr.	før Kristus
	2 direktorat	fl.	flaske
	3 direktør	flg.	følgende
	4 dirigent	flt.	flertal
div.	1 diverse	fm.	1 formiddag
	2 division		2 fuldmægtig
DM	danmarksmesterskab	f.m.	foregående måned
do.	ditto	fmd.	formand
dr.	1 doctor, e.g. dr.phil.	f.o.m.	fra og med
	2 doktor	forb.	1 forbindelse
	3 drenge		2 forbud
d.s.	1 den/det/de samme	foreg.	foregående
	2 dennes	forf.	forfatter
d.s.s.	det samme som	fork.	forkortelse, forkortet
dvs.	det vil sige	forsk.	forskellig
d.y.	den yngre	forts.	fortsættelse, fortsættes
d.æ.	den ældre	FP	førtidspension
d.å.	dette år	fr.	1 fredag
edb	elektronisk		2 fru, frøken
	databehandling	frk.	frøken
eftf.	efterfølger	f.t.	for tiden
egl.	egentlig	f.v.t.	før vor tidsregning
e.Kr.	efter Kristus	fx	for eksempel
eks.	eksempel	f.å.	foregående år
ekskl.	eksklusive	g	1 gram
ekspl.	eksemplar		2 gymnasieklasse
e.l.	eller lignende	g., gg.	gang(e)
enk.	enkelt	gl.	1 gammel
EM	europamesterskab		2 glas
em.	eftermiddag	g.m.	gift med
etc.	etcetera	gnsn.	gennemsnit
evt.	eventuel (-t, -le)	gr.	1 grad
f.	1 femininum		2 gruppe
	2 for	G/S, g/s	gensidigt selskab

GT	Gamle Testamente	K/S, k/s	kommanditselskab
ha	hektar	kt.	konto
henv.	1 henvendelse	kv.	kvinde(lig)
	2 henvisning	l	liter
hf	højere	l.	linie, linje
	forberedelseseksamen	lb.nr.	løbenummer
hhv.	henholdsvis	lejl.	lejlighed
hk	hestekraft	lign.	lignende
H.K.H.	Hans/Hendes	Ll.	Lille (in place names)
	Kongelige	lok.	1 lokal(nummer)
	Højhed		2 lokale
hpl.	holdeplads	lø.	lørdag
hr.	herre	m.	med
i alm.	i almindelighed	ma.	mandag
ib.	indbundet	m.a.o.	med andre ord
if.	ifølge	mc	1 motorcykel
i henh. til	i henhold til		2 musikkassette
iht.	i henhold til	md.	måned
indb.	1 indbundet	mdl.	1 mandlig
	2 indbygger		2 månedlig
ing.	ingeniør	mdtl.	mundligt
inkl.	inklusive	medd.	meddelelse
instr.	1 instruktion,	medflg.	medfølgende
	instruktør	medl.	medlem
	2 instrument	MF	medlem af Folketinget
I/S, i/s	interessentselskab	mfl., m.fl.	med flere
istf., i st.	i stedet for	mgl.	mangler, manglende
for		mhp.,	med henblik på
itk.	intetkøn	m.h.p.	
jan.	januar	mht., m.h.t.	med hensyn til
jf. (jvf.)	jævnfør	mia.	milliard(er)
j. nr.	journalnummer	mio.	million(er)
kap.	kapitel	m/k	mand(lig)/kvinde(lig)
kat.	1 katalog	ml.	mellem
	2 katolsk	m.m.	med mere
kbh.	københavnsk	modsv.	modsvarende
kgl.	kongelig	modt.	modtager
kl.	1 klasse	mv., m.v.	med videre
	2 klokken	N	nord
kld.	kælder	n.	neutrum
km/t.	kilometer i timen	ndf.	nedenfor
Kr.	Kirke (in place names)	ned.	nederst
kr.	krone(r)	nedenst.	nedenstående

NM	nordisk mesterskab	par.	paragraf
NN	nomen nescio (=I do not know the name.)	p.b.v.	på bestyrelsens vegne
		pct.	procent
		pga, p.g.a.	på grund af
nord.	nordisk	pk.	pakke
nov.	november	pkt.	punkt
Nr.	Nørre (in place names)	Pl.	Plads (in place names)
		pl., plur.	pluralis
nr.	nummer	P&T	post- og telegrafvæsenet
NT	Ny Testamente		
nto.	netto	pr.	per
nuv.	nuværende	pt.	patient
o.	omkring	p.t.	pro tempore (for the time being)
o.a.	og andet/andre		
obl.	obligatorisk	p ... v.	på ...s vegne
obs!	observer!	på gr. af	på grund af
off.	1 offentlig 2 officiel	R	rekommanderet (letters)
ofl., o.fl.	og flere	rad.	radikal
og lign.	og lignende	red.	redaktion, redaktør, redigeret (af)
okt.	oktober		
OL	Olympiske Lege	regn.	regning
o.l.	og lignende	repr.	repræsentant
o/m	omdrejninger per minut	resp.	respektive
		S	syd
o.m.a.	og mange andre, og meget andet	s	sekund
		s.	side
omg.	1 omgang 2 omgående	sa.	samme
		s.d.	se denne (dette, disse)
omkr.	omkring	Sdr.	Sønder, Søndre (in place names)
omr.	område		
omtr.	omtrent	sept.	september
ons.	onsdag	sg.	singularis
opg.	opgang	s/h	sort-hvid
opl.	1 oplag 2 oplysning	sing.	singularis
		Skt.	Sankt
opr.	1 oprettet 2 oprindelig	s.m.	samme måned
		sml.	sammenlign
ovenn.	ovennævnte	sn	sogn
ovenst.	ovenstående	spec.	specielt
ovf.	ovenfor	spm.	spørgsmål
p-	parkerings-, præventiv(pille)	spsk.	spiseskefuld
		St.	Store (in place names)

st.	1 station	uafh.	uafhængig
	2 stuen (etage)	udb., udbet.	udbetaling
	3 størrelse	udg.	udgave, udgivet (af)
stk.	styk(ke)	uds.	udsendelse
s.u.	svar udbedes	undt.	undtagen
sædv.	sædvanlig(vis)	u.å.	uden år
søn.	søndag	V	vest
s.å.	samme år	V.	Vester (in place
t	ton		names)
t.	time	v.	ved
tdl.	tønde(r) land	vedr.	vedrørende
t.eks.	til eksempel	vejl.	vejledning
th., t.h.	til højre	VM	verdensmesterskab
tidl.	tidligere	vvs	varme, ventilation,
tilh.	tilhørende		sanitet
tilsv.	tilsvarende	vær.	værelse
tirs.	tirsdag	Ø	øst
tlf.	telefon	Ø.	Øster (in place names)
tors.	torsdag	øv.	øverst
t.o.m.	til og med	øvr.	øvrige
tsk.	teskefuld	årg.	årgang
tv., t.v.	til venstre	årh.	århundrede
u.	1 uden	årl.	årlig
	2 under		

13 ORTHOGRAPHY

166 THE ALPHABET

The Danish alphabet contains the same letters as the English alphabet, but after **z** come three additional letters: **Æ/æ**, **Ø/ø** and **Å/å** in that order. The letters **c**, **q**, **w** and **x** are less commonly used in Danish and are usually found only in loanwords. The spelling reform of 1948 saw three important changes:

1 The letter **Å/å** was introduced.
2 The capital letter at the beginning of nouns (as in German) was abolished.
3 The modals **kunde**, **skulde**, **vilde** became **kunne**, **skulle**, **ville** (could, should, would).

167 Aa, Å, aa, å

When, in 1948, Denmark officially replaced the spelling **Aa** and **aa** with the letters **Å** and **å** in most words, words such as **aaben** and **paastaa** became **åben** (open) and **påstå** (claim). This change in spelling did not affect pronunciation.

This reform brought Danish spelling into line with spelling in Norway and Sweden. There was initially resistance on the part of some towns, institutions and individuals, so that spellings such as **Aabenraa** or **Aage Skovgaard** are still found. Individuals may retain the older spelling whilst local authorities legally have to use the new ones. Strangely, the position of this new letter in the alphabet was not officially determined until 1955. In fact, it moved from the beginning to the end of the Danish alphabet (which now begins with A and ends with Å), causing a lot of work for lexicographers.

168 SMALL OR CAPITAL LETTERS?

1 Where English has a capital letter at the beginning of words, in many cases Danish has a small letter, such as:

- Days of the week, months and festivals:

    tirsdag, Tuesday; **juni**, June; **påske**, Easter

- Nationality words (both nouns and adjectives):

    dansk, Danish; **engelsk**, English; **finsk**, Finnish; **en amerikaner**, an American; **en franskmand**, a Frenchman; **en tysker**, a German

2 Proper nouns (names) constituting a single word have a capital letter:

Var Diderichsen dansker?   Was Diderichsen a Dane?

3 In compound names the first element of the compound has a capital letter but the second element loses its capital:

Storlkøbenhavn, Greater Copenhagen   cf. **København**, Copenhagen

Note that in some compounds which have become fixed expressions the first element may lose its capital letter:

et danmarklslkort, a map of Denmark, cf. **Danmark**, Denmark
or: **et Danmarklslkort**

4 In name phrases the first and other significant words tend to have capital letters:

Forenede Nationer, the United Nations; **Gorm den Gamle**, King Gorm the Old; **Dansk Kirke i Udlandet**, the Danish Church in Foreign Ports

If the name is introduced by a definite article, the article may or may not have a capital letter:

Det/det Kongelige Teater, The Royal Theatre; **De/de Kanariske Øer**, The Canary Islands; also with an addition **Det/det nye Kongelige Bibliotek**, The new Royal Library.

169 WORD DIVISION

Sometimes it is necessary to divide words at the end of lines, and this word division (or hyphenation) in Danish follows some basic principles:

1 Compounds are divided into their separate elements:

møbel-fabrik, gå-gade, halv-år

2 Derivatives may be divided according to prefix or suffix:

u-vane, af-folke, musik-ant, arbejd-som

3 Inflexional endings that constitute a syllable can be divided from the stem:

huse-ne, lav-ere, svare-de

4 There must be at least one vowel on each line. Thus a single syllable word cannot be divided, e.g. **blomst, mindst, strengt**.

5 Words which are neither compounds nor derivatives divide according to the number of consonants involved:

(a) One or two consonants – one consonant goes on the new line:

bo-gen, **bus-sen**

(b) A consonant group may move to the new line if it can begin a Danish word.

bis-pen or **bi-spen**, **tas-ke** or **ta-ske**

(c) Consonants in the same syllable cannot be separated:

*kno-gle	BUT	**knog-le**
*te-knik	BUT	**tek-nik**

14 PUNCTUATION

170 PUNCTUATION MARKS

The names of the principal punctuation marks (**skilletegn**) used in Danish are:

.	**punktum**
,	**komma**
:	**kolon**
;	**semikolon**
?	**spørgsmålstegn**
!	**udråbstegn**
/	**skråstreg**
-	**bindestreg**
–	**tankestreg**
'	**apostrof**
...	**prikker**
( )	**parentes**
[ ]	**firkantet parentes**
{ }	**klammer**
" "/„ "/' '/» «	**anførselstegn**

171 THE COMMA

For some time Danish has had two different systems of using the comma. One, called the 'traditional comma', was clause-based and was applied mechanically to the text; the other, known as the 'pause comma', was used to indicate natural pauses in the text.

In 1996, *Dansk Sprognævn* (the Danish National Language Council) attempted to combine the two systems. However, the outcome was (i) that the 'traditional comma' was preserved but renamed the 'grammatical comma', and (ii) that a new system, the 'new comma', was devised which is closer to the previous 'pause comma'.

But although there are thus still two acceptable comma systems in Danish, *Dansk Sprognævn* itself strongly recommends the use of the 'new comma', and therefore this is the system outlined below.

1 The comma is used:

(a) Between two coordinated clauses:

Det sner, og det er koldt.   It is snowing and it is cold.

(b) Between a subordinate clause and a following main clause:

Da vi havde spist, gik vi i byen.   When we had eaten we went into town.

(c) Around a non-restrictive relative clause (cf. **75**) or another parenthetical expression:

Min far, som nu er meget gammel, bor på Falster.
My father, who is now very old, lives on Falster.

(d) After (but not before) a restrictive relative clause (cf. **75**):

Folk der kommer for sent, må vente udenfor.
People who are late must wait outside.

(e) To mark a parenthetical apposition:

Danmarks nordligste punkt, Grenen, ligger ved Skagen.
The northernmost point in Denmark, Grenen, is near Skagen.

(f) To mark elements in the extra position (cf. **141**):

Peter, ham kan du godt stole på.   Peter, him you can trust.

(g) To mark off interjections (cf. **132**):

Ja, det har du ret i.   Yes, you are right there.

(h) To mark enumerations, though not the last one after **og**:

Han købte kød, frugt, brød og vin.   He bought meat, fruit, bread and wine.

(i) Before **men**:

Vi læser avis, men hører ikke radio.
We read the paper but don't listen to the radio.

2 There is no comma:

(a) Between a main clause and a following subordinate clause:

Hun sagde at hun var træt.   She said she was tired.

(b) Before a restrictive relative clause (cf. **75**):

Jeg læste den bog som du gav mig.   I read the book that you gave me.

(c) Around non-parenthetic apposition:

Den berømte danske romanforfatter Peter Høeg taler her i dag.
The famous Danish novelist Peter Høeg is speaking here today.

In 2 (a) and (b), the 'grammatical comma' system would have required a comma: (a) before **at**, (b) before **som**.

172 THE FULL STOP

The full stop is found:

1 At the end of a sentence:

Kampen blev udsat til den følgende søndag.
The match was postponed until the following Sunday.

2 In some abbreviations (cf. **165**):

bl.a., inter alia; **f.eks.**, e.g.; **m.m.**, etc.

3 In mathematical expressions (cf. **65**):

1.000.000 kr   1,000,000 kroner

Note that Danish uses a decimal comma, where English has a decimal point (**65.5**):

7,5 l   7.5 litres

173 THE EXCLAMATION MARK

The exclamation mark is used when addressing people directly, and after exclamations and rhetorical questions:

Mine damer og herrer!	Ladies and gentlemen!
Hej!	Hi!
På gensyn, Helle!	See you soon, Helle!
Du er komplet åndssvag!	You are completely insane!

174 DIRECT SPEECH

Several different typographical conventions are used to indicate dialogue:

(a) dash (**tankestreg**)	**– Hvad hedder du? spurgte han.** 'What's your name?' he asked.
(b) inverted commas	**"Er der noget på færde?" spurgte hun.** 'Is something wrong?' she asked.
(c) guillemet	**»Hvor er du, Peter?« kaldte hans mor.** 'Where are you, Peter?' his mother called.

175   THE APOSTROPHE

1 Unlike in English, the apostrophe is not normally used to indicate a possessor (i.e. to mark a genitive):

kattens hale	the cat's tail
Gretes onkel	Grete's uncle

2 Note, however, that the apostrophe is found indicating a genitive after proper nouns ending in **-s**, **-x**, **-z** (see also **37.3**):

Lars'(s) kusiner	Lars's cousins
Marx'(s) skrifter	Marx's writings

3 The apostrophe is sometimes used to mark an inflexional ending:

(a) In abbreviations without a full stop:

pc'en, the PC (personal computer); **tv'et**, the TV set; **wc'er**, toilets

(b) After numerals:

1990'erne, the 1990s

176   THE HYPHEN

The hyphen is used:

1 to replace **og**:

engelsk-dansk ordbog, English–Danish dictionary

2 To replace **(fra)** ... **til**:

Butikken er åben 9–18. The shop is open 9 to 6.

3 To avoid repetition of the second element of a compound:

rug- eller franskbrød, rye bread or French bread
(← rugbrød eller franskbrød)

4 Where the first element of a compound is an abbreviation or a number:

p-plads, parking place; **2000-tallet**, the 21st century

LINGUISTIC TERMS

This list comprises terms that may not be familiar to a student of languages, as well as those that are not already explained in the text. Users should also consult the Index for references in the text.

ABSTRACT NOUNS refer to unobservable notions, e.g. **musik**, music; **påstand**, assertion; **vanskelighed**, difficulty.

ABSTRACT SENSE is when the literal sense is no longer transparent. Compare the meaning of the verb in: **Hun satte kartoflerne over**, She put the potatoes on (literal sense) with: **Hun oversatte bogen**, She translated the book (abstract sense); (cf. FIGURATIVE SENSE).

ADJECTIVE PHRASES consist of an adjective or a participle with one or more modifiers, e.g. **Han er *utrolig energisk***, He is incredibly energetic.

ADVERB PHRASES consist of an adverb with one or more modifiers, e.g. **Han kørte *temmelig hurtigt***, He drove quite fast.

ADVERBIALS (see CLAUSAL ADVERBS) are words, phrases or clauses that function as adverbs. Adverbs, noun phrases, prepositional phrases and subordinate clauses can all be adverbials of different kinds (manner, place, time, condition, etc.), e.g. **Hun sang *smukt*** (adverb, manner), She sang beautifully; **Hun sang *hele aftenen*** (noun phrase, time), She sang the whole evening; **Hun sang *i Det Kongelige Teater*** (prep. phrase, place), She sang in the Royal Theatre; **Hun sang kun *hvis hun havde lyst*** (sub. clause, condition), She only sang when she felt like it.

AFFIX is a prefix added to the beginning or a suffix added to the end of a word, e.g. ***u*lykkelig**, unhappy; **god*hed***, goodness.

AGENT is the person or thing carrying out the action in both active and passive constructions, e.g. ***Drengen* stjæler bilen**, The boy steals the car; **Bilen stjæles *af drengen***, The car is stolen by the boy.

AGREEMENT is a way of showing that two grammatical units have a certain feature in common, e.g. **min*e* hund*e***, my dogs; **Slott*et* er stor*t***, The castle is big.

APPOSITION is where two consecutive noun phrases, separated only by a comma, describe the same entity, e.g. ***Per, min bror,* er rig**, Per, my brother, is rich.

ATTRIBUTIVE is used to describe adjectives or pronouns that precede a noun and modify it, e.g. **et *stort* hus**, a big house; ***min* bil**, my car.

BLENDS are new words formed by omitting part of an existing word, e.g. **merværdiomsætningsafgift** → *moms*, VAT.

CLAUSAL ADVERBS are adverbs that modify the sense of the clause as a whole, e.g. **Han er *ikke* dum**, He's not stupid; **De er *altid* ude**, They are always out.

CLAUSE is a syntactic unit that usually consists of at least a finite verb and a subject (though the subject may be understood, as in most imperative clauses, e.g. **Hent lige avisen!**, Do fetch the paper, please!). There are two major types of clause: main clauses (MC) and subordinate clauses (SC), e.g. **Middagen stod på bordet** (MC) **da jeg kom hjem** (SC), The dinner was on the table when I got home (cf. SENTENCE).

CLIPPINGS are new words formed by omitting the beginning or end of a word, e.g. **automobil** → *bil*, car; **biograf** → *bio*, cinema.

COLLECTIVE NOUNS are nouns whose singular form denotes a group, e.g. **familie**, family; **hold**, team; **kvæg**, cattle.

COMMON NOUNS are all nouns that are not PROPER NOUNS, e.g. **en hund**, a dog; **to borde**, two tables.

COMPLEMENTS express a meaning that adds to (or complements) that of the subject or object. They can be either an ADJECTIVE (PHRASE) or a NOUN (PHRASE), e.g. **Dorthe og Sven er *intelligente*. De er *gode venner***, Dorthe and Sven are intelligent. They are good friends; **De slog ham *bevidstløs***, They knocked him unconscious. (For 'prepositional complement' see PREPOSITIONAL PHRASE.)

COMPLEX VERBS have two or more parts: **Jeg *har spist* snegle**, I have eaten snails; **Cyklen *er blevet stjålet***, The bike has been stolen.

COMPOUND VERBS are verbs consisting of a STEM and a prefix or particle, which may be inseparable or separable from the stem, e.g. *be*tale, pay, but *de*ltage/tage *del*, take part.

CONJUGATION denotes the way a verb is inflected, i.e. its pattern of endings, and the grouping of verbs according to their endings, e.g. past tense forms in: Conj. I **leve – levede**, live; Conj. II **spise – spiste**, eat.

COPULAS are verbs linking a subject complement to the subject, e.g. *Pia er* dansker, Pia is a Dane; **Søren *blev* sur**, Søren became bad-tempered.

CORRELATIVE is the word or phrase that a pronoun replaces or refers to, e.g. **Den tale** is replaced by **som** in: **Den tale som han holdt, var kedelig**, The speech that he made was boring.

COUNT NOUNS are nouns that denote individual countable entities and therefore usually have a plural form (including zero-ending), e.g. **bog – bøger**, book-s; **dreng – drenge**, boy-s; **æg – æg**, egg-s.

DECLENSION denotes the different ways of INFLECTING count nouns in the plural, e.g. **bil*er***, **krig*e***, **flag**, cars, wars, flags. It also denotes adjective inflexion, e.g. **en rød bil**, a red car; **et rød*t* hus**, a red house; **den rø*de* bil**, the red car.

DEFINITE refers to a specified entity, cf. *Tyven* **har stjålet cyklen**, The thief has stolen the bike. Indefinite refers to a non-specified entity, e.g. *En tyv* **har stjålet cyklen**, A thief has stolen the bike.

DERIVATIVE refers to a word derived from a STEM, usually by the addition of an AFFIX, e.g. **angå**, concern; **foregå**, take place; and **overgå**, surpass; are all derivatives of the verb **gå**, go.

DIRECT OBJECT denotes a noun phrase, a pronoun or a clause governed by a (transitive) verb, e.g. **Drengen hentede** *bolden/den,* The boy fetched the ball/it; **Hun sagde** *at hun var træt,* She said that she was tired.

DUPLICATION involves the repetition of a subject, object or adverbial, usually in the form of a pronoun or adverb, e.g. *Jens, han* **er ikke dum**, Jens, he isn't stupid.

ELLIPSIS involves the omission of a word or word group in the sentence, e.g. **Må jeg få en is? Nej, du må ikke** */få en is/*, Can I have an ice cream? No, you can't/have an ice cream/.

FIGURATIVE SENSE is when the literal sense has been extended but is still somehow transparent, e.g. **Han fulgte i sin faders fodspor**, He followed in his father's footsteps (cf. ABSTRACT SENSE).

FINITE VERB is a verb form which in itself shows tense (and sometimes mood and/or voice). There are three finite verb forms in Danish: the present tense, the past tense and the imperative, e.g. **Jeg venter**; **Jeg ventede**; **Vent!**, I'm waiting; I waited; Wait! (cf. NON-FINITE VERB).

FORMAL SUBJECT is **der** or **det** in cases when the REAL SUBJECT is postponed, e.g. *Der* (FS) **sidder en gammel mand** (RS) **på bænken**, There's an old man sitting on the bench; *Det* (FS) **er synd at du ikke kan komme til festen** (RS), It's a pity that you can't come to the party.

FRONT is the position at the beginning of a main clause. It is usually occupied by the subject, e.g. *Vi* **er sultne**, We are hungry. But non-subjects, especially ADVERBIAL expressions of time or place, often occupy the front position, e.g. *I morgen* **skal jeg spille fodbold**, Tomorrow I'm playing football.

GENDER may indicate sex: **drengen** – *han*; **pigen** – *hun*, the boy – he; the girl – she; or grammatical gender: *et* **barn**, a child; *et* **hus**, a house; *en* **stol**, a chair.

IDIOM(ATIC) indicates a traditional usage that is not readily explicable from the grammar or from the individual elements.

IMPERATIVE is a finite verb form identical in Danish with the stem of the verb, expressing a command, warning, direction or the like, e.g. **Kom!**, Come on!; **Vend om!**, Turn round!

IMPERSONAL CONSTRUCTIONS do not involve a person but usually **det** or **der**, e.g. **Det sner**, It's snowing; **Der snydes meget**, There's a lot of cheating.

INDECLINABLE describes words that do not INFLECT, e.g. the adjectives **moderne**, good; **fælles**, common, mutual; which take no endings for gender or plural: **et moderne hus**, a modern house; **fælles venner**, mutual friends. Whole word classes may be indeclinable, e.g. conjunctions and prepositions.

INDEFINITE (see DEFINITE)

INDIRECT OBJECT usually denotes a person or an animal benefiting from an action (i.e. the recipient), e.g. **Vi gav _ham_ pengene**, We gave him the money.

INFINITIVE PHRASE is a phrase consisting of an infinitive accompanied by one or more modifiers, e.g. **at skrive et brev**, to write a letter.

INFLECT means to change the form of a word by means of endings, vowel changes or in other ways, e.g. the verb **skrive**, write, inflects **skriv**, **skrive**, **skriv**_er_, **skrev**, **skrev**_et_, etc.

INFLEXION (see INFLECT)

INTERROGATIVE is used of questions, e.g. interrogative pronouns and adverbs introduce a question: **_Hvem_ var det?**, Who was that?; **_Hvorfor_ kom du ikke?**, Why didn't you come?

INVERTED word order denotes verb – subject order, e.g. **I dag _rejser vi_**, Today we are leaving.

MATRIX is that part of a complex sentence that remains when the subordinate clause is removed, e.g. **_Birthe lovede_ at hun ville skrive til os**, Birthe promised that she would write to us.

MORPHEME is the smallest part of a word expressing meaning: in the word **bilerne**, the cars, there are three morphemes: **_bil_**, car, **_er_** (plural morpheme), **_ne_** (definite plural morpheme).

MUTATED VOWEL is one that changes when a word is inflected, e.g. $o \rightarrow ø$ in **fod** – **fødder**, foot – feet; $u \rightarrow y$ in **_ung_** – **_yngre_**, young – younger.

NOMINAL means a word or phrase functioning as a noun, e.g. **_Bogen_ er interessant**, The book is interesting; **_At læse_ er interessant**, Reading is interesting.

NON-COUNT NOUNS are nouns that cannot describe individual countable entities. They may be either singular words with no plural form, usually denoting substances (mass-words), e.g. **luft**, air; **mel**, flour; **sand**, sand; or they may be plural words with no equivalent singular form, e.g. **klæder**, clothes; **penge**, money; **shorts**, shorts.

NON-FINITE VERB forms are those not showing tense, namely the infinitive and the participles, e.g. **(at) løbe**, (to) run; **løbende**, running; **løbet**, run.

NOUN PHRASES consist of a noun accompanied by one or more modifiers which may precede or follow the noun, e.g. **en dejlig dag**, a lovely day; **en dag som jeg aldrig vil glemme**, a day I shall never forget.

NUMBER is a collective term for singular and plural. The plural form is usually marked by an inflexional ending, e.g. **en blyant**, a pencil; **to blyant**_er_, two pencils.

PART OF SPEECH means word class, e.g. noun, adjective, verb, conjunction, etc.

PARTICLE is a stressed adverb or preposition appearing together with a verb to form a single unit of meaning, e.g. **ned** in **skrive _ned_**, write down; **ud** in **skælde _ud_**, tell off.

PARTITIVE denotes a part of a whole or of a substance, e.g. *en del af* **pengene**, some of the money; *en flaske* **vin**, a bottle of wine; *et kilo* **kartofler**, a kilo of potatoes.

PEJORATIVE means deprecating, e.g. **dit fjols!**, you idiot!

PREDICATE is the central part of the clause, excluding the subject. The predicate comprises the verb plus any object, complement or adverbial: **Han** *spiller (klaver hver dag)*, He plays (the piano every day).

PREDICATIVE indicates the position after a copula verb: **Skuespillet er** *svært*, The play is difficult; **De bliver** *gamle*, They're growing old.

PREDICATIVE COMPLEMENT is a noun (phrase) or adjective (phrase) in the PREDICATE complementing (i.e. filling out) the subject or object: **Leo er** *min bror.* **Han er** *seks år gammel*, Leo is my brother. He is six years old.

PREPOSITIONAL PHRASE consists of a preposition plus a prepositional complement (a noun (phrase), a pronoun, an infinitive (phrase) or a clause), e.g. **pigen** *med det lange hår*, the girl with the long hair; **pigen tænkte** *på ham*, the girl thought of him; **pigen gik** *uden at sige farvel*, the girl left without saying goodbye; **pigen sørgede for** *at bordet blev dækket*, the girl saw to it that the table was set.

PRODUCTIVE implies that a word class or method of word formation can still produce new words, e.g. the suffix **-bar** in **vaskbar**, washable.

PROPER NOUNS are names of specific people, places, occasions, events, books, etc., e.g. **Jørgen**, **Randers**, *Løgneren*.

REAL SUBJECT is the postponed subject, e.g. **Det er dejligt** *at drikke vin*, It's nice to drink wine (cf. FORMAL SUBJECT).

RECIPROCAL indicates a mutual activity expressed either in the pronoun, e.g. **De elsker** *hinanden*, They love each other; or in the verb, e.g. **Vi** *ses* **i morgen**, See you tomorrow.

SEMANTIC denotes the meaning of words, phrases, etc.

SENTENCE is a syntactic unit that contains a complete meaning and consists of one or more clauses (cf. CLAUSE). Thus the following three examples are all sentences: **Se der!**, Look there!; **Hun tager bussen når det regner**, She takes the bus when it rains; **Hvis du tror at jeg kan huske hvad han sagde da vi besøgte ham i sidste uge, tager du fejl**, If you think that I can remember what he said when we visited him last week, you're wrong.

SIMPLE VERBS consist of one word only (a FINITE VERB), e.g. *Hjælp!*, Help!; **(han)** *sover*, (he) sleeps; **(han)** *gik*, (he) went.

STATEMENT is a sentence or clause conveying information, as distinct from a question, exclamation or command.

STEM is the part of the verb onto which inflexional endings are added, e.g. **danse**, **dans*er***, **dans*ede***, **dans*et***.

SYLLABLE consists of a vowel and usually one or more consonants, e.g. **ø, dø, rør, rødt, in-du-stri-ar-bej-de-re**.

TAG QUESTION is a phrase attached to the end of a statement which turns it into a question: **Han kan lide laks,** *ikke sandt?*, He likes salmon, doesn't he?

VERB PHRASES consist of a FINITE VERB form (optionally) accompanied by one or more NON-FINITE VERB forms in a chain, e.g. **Han** *sover*, He is sleeping; **Han** *må kunne løbe*, He must be able to run.

DANISH, LATIN AND ENGLISH LINGUISTIC TERMS

In many Danish grammars and works on language, Danish linguistic terms are used in preference to the more international Latin-based terms. This list shows equivalents.

Danish	Latin	English
Selvlyd	Vokal	Vowel
Medlyd	Konsonant	Consonant
Navneord	Substantiv	Noun
Egennavn	Proprium	Proper noun
Kendeord	Artikel	Article
Tillægsord	Adjektiv	Adjective
Stedord	Pronomen	Pronoun
Personligt stedord	Personligt pronomen	Personal pronoun
Ejestedord	Possessivt pronomen	Possessive pronoun
Tilbagevisende stedord	Refleksivt pronomen	Reflexive pronoun
Gensidigt stedord	Reciprokt pronomen	Reciprocal pronoun
Påpegende stedord	Demonstrativt pronomen	Demonstrative pronoun
Spørgende stedord	Interrogativt pronomen	Interrogative pronoun
Henførende stedord	Relativt pronomen	Relative pronoun
Ubestemt stedord	Indefinit pronomen	Indefinite pronoun
Talord	Numerale	Numeral
Mængdetal	Kardinaltal	Cardinal number
Ordenstal	Ordinaltal	Ordinal number
Udsagnsord	Verbum	Verb
Mådesudsagnsord	Modalverbum	Modal verb
Biord	Adverbium	Adverb
Bindeord	Konjunktion	Conjunction
Forholdsord	Præposition	Preposition
Ytringsord	Interjektion	Interjection
Fald	Kasus	Case
Grundledsfald	Nominativ	Nominative
Genstandsfald	Akkusativ/dativ	Accusative/dative
Tillægsfald	Genitiv	Genitive

Danish	*Latin*	*English*
Tal	**Numerus**	Number
Ental	**Singular**	Singular
Flertal	**Pluralis**	Plural
Køn	**Genus**	Gender
Fælleskøn	**Commune**	Common gender
	(maskulinum/femininum)	(masculine/feminine)
Intetkøn	**Neutrum**	Neuter
Gradbøjning	**Komparation**	Comparison
1 **grad**	**Positiv**	Positive
2 **grad**	**Komparativ**	Comparative
3 **grad**	**Superlativ**	Superlative
Måde	**Modus**	Mood
Fortællemåde	**Indikativ**	Indicative
Bydemåde	**Imperativ**	Imperative
Ønskemåde	**Konjunktiv**	Subjunctive
Tid	**Tempus**	Tense
Art	**Diatese = aktiv/passiv**	active/passive voice
Navneform	**Infinitiv**	Infinitive
Tillægsform	**Participium**	Participle
Forstavelse	**Præfiks**	Prefix
(Aflednings)endelse	**Suffiks**	Suffix
Navnesamstilling	**Apposition**	Apposition
Udsagnsled	**Verbal(led)**	(Finite) Verb
Grundled	**Subjekt**	Subject
Genstandsled	**Objekt**	Object
Omsagnsled	**Prædikativ**	Complement
Biled	**Adverbial**	Adverbial
Sideordning	**Paratakse**	Parataxis
Underordning	**Hypotakse**	Hypotaxis
Samordning	**Neksus**	Nexus

Supplementary terms

A **Sætningsdannende verbalformer**	**Finitte verbalformer**	Finite verb forms
1 **Nutidsform**	**Præsens**	Present tense
2 **Datidsform**	**Imperfektum/ Præteritum**	Past tense
3 **Bydeform**	**Imperativ**	Imperative
4 **Ønskeform**	**Konjunktiv**	Subjunctive
B **Ikke-sætnings- dannende verbal- former**	**Infinitte verbalformer**	Non-finite verb forms
1 **Navneform**	**Infinitiv**	Infinitive

2 **Tillægsform**	**Participium**	Participle
a **Nutids tillægsform**	**Præsens participium**	Present participle
b **Datids tillægsform**	**Perfektum/Præteritum participium**	Past participle
Ubøjet	**Verbalt participium**	Verbal participle
Bøjelig	**Adjektivisk participium**	Adjectival participle

SHORT BIBLIOGRAPHY

Unless otherwise stated, works are published in Copenhagen.

Afzelius, Otto *et al.*, *Dansk grammatik for udlændinge*, 8th ed., Special-pædagogisk Forlag, Herning, 1986.

Allan, Robin, Philip Holmes and Tom Lundskær-Nielsen, *Danish: A Comprehensive Grammar*, Routledge, London, 1995 [1998].

Becker-Christensen, Christian and Peter Widell, *Politikens Nudansk Grammatik*, Politikens Forlag, 1995.

Brink, Lars *et al.*, *Den Store Danske Udtaleordbog*, Munksgaard, 1991.

Dansk Sprognævn, *Danske Dobbeltformer. Valgfri former i retskrivningen*, ed. H. Galberg Jacobsen, Munksgaard, 1992.

Diderichsen, Paul, *Elementær dansk grammatik*, 3rd ed., Gyldendal, 1962.

Eriksen, Jørgen and Arne Hamburger, *Forkortelser i hverdagen*, Gyldendal, 1988.

Fischer-Hansen, Barbara and Ann Kledal, *Grammatikken – håndbog i dansk grammatik for udlændinge*, Special-pædagogisk Forlag, Herning, 1994.

Grønnum, Nina, *Fonetik og Fonologi. Almen og Dansk*, Akademisk Forlag, 1998.

Hansen, Erik, *Skrift, stavning og retstavning*, 2nd ed., Hans Reitzel, 1991.

Hansen, Erik, *Rigtigt dansk*, 2nd ed., Hans Reitzel, 1993.

Hansen, Erik, *Dæmonernes Port. Støttemateriale til undervisningen i nydansk*, 4th ed., Hans Reitzel, 1997.

Hansen, Aage, *Moderne dansk I-III*, Grafisk Forlag, 1967.

Jacobsen, Henrik Galberg, *Erhvervsdansk. Opslagsbog*, Schønberg, 1990.

Jacobsen, Henrik Galberg, *Sæt nyt komma. Regler, grammatik, genveje og øvelser*, Dansklærerforeningen, 1996.

Jacobsen, Henrik Galberg and Peder Skyum-Nielsen, *Erhvervsdansk. Grundbog,* Schønberg, 1990.

Jacobsen, Henrik Galberg and Peder Skyum-Nielsen, *Dansk sprog. En grundbog*, Schønberg, 1996.

Jacobsen, Henrik Galberg and Peter Stray Jørgensen, *Politikens Basisbog om Dansk Sprogbrug*, Politikens Forlag, 1996.

Jacobsen, Henrik Galberg and Peter Stray Jørgensen, *Håndbog i Nudansk*, 3rd ed., Politikens Forlag, 1997.

Jarvad, Pia, *Nye ord – hvorfor og hvordan?*, Gyldendal, 1995.

Jones, W. Glyn and Kirsten Gade, *Danish. A Grammar*, Gyldendal, 1981.

Lomholt, Jørgen, *Le Danois Contemporain*, Akademisk Forlag, 1982.

Nordentoft, Annelise Munck, *Hovedtræk af dansk grammatik. Ordklasser*, 2nd ed., Gyldendal, 1972.

Nordentoft, Annelise Munck, *Hovedtræk af dansk grammatik. Syntaks*, 3rd ed., Gyldendal, 1982.

Petersen, Pia Riber, *Nye ord i dansk 1955–1975*, Gyldendal, 1984.

Politikens Store Nye Nudansk Ordbog, Politikens Forlag, 1996.

Retskrivningsordbogen, 2nd ed., Aschehoug, 1996.

Sørensen, Knud, *Engelsk i dansk. Er det et must?*, Munksgaard, 1995.

Vinterberg, Hermann and C.A. Bodelsen, *Dansk-Engelsk Ordbog*, 4th ed., ed. V. Hjørnager Pedersen, Gyldendal, 1998.

INDEX

Figures refer to *paragraphs* and *sub-paragraphs*. Words in bold are Danish. Words in italics are English.

AA/aa 166f
abbreviation 164f
about 127
above 127
abstract nouns 34
acronym 164.3
active verb 105
ad 113
adjectival noun 54, 93.3(b)
adjective 44–63
adjective agreement 44, 51f
adverb 107–11
adverbial, *see:* Clausal adverbial,
  Other adverbials
adverbial clause 154
adverbs of location and motion 110
af 114
affix 163
affixation 163
after 127
against 127
agent 105.2, 148, 152, 155
agreement 44, 51f
al (alt, alle) 78
aldrig 160.3
altid 107.3
amplifier 113
anden (andet, andre) 64.1
apostrophe 175
article 38
article use 39–43
as 136.2
as ... as 136.3
ask 81.5, 85.1
at 127ff
at (conjunction) 134.2(a), 135.8, 156.3
at (infinitive marker) 91.2
at- clause with a 'topic' 159.1
at- clause with FV-CA word order
  159.2
auxiliary verb 92.2, 143

bare 134.2(b)
barn 28.1, 29.3
be 88.3
before 127, 136.4
begge 135.5
below 127
blend 164.2
blive (bliver, blev, blevet) 10, 86.3
blive passive 105.5
blå 48.2
borrowing 161.1
bort 110.2
borte 110.2
both 136.5
burde (bør, burde) 100
but 136.6
by 127
både ... og 135.4

can 100
capital letter 168
cardinal number 64f
century 65.6
clausal adverbial 107, 145, 151, 156.1,
  160.2, 160.3
clause element 137
clause stress 14f
clause structure 137–60
clause types 138
cleft sentence 158
clipping 164.1
clock 66
collective 33.2n, 35
come 90.3
comma 171
command 101.2, 138.2, 139
common abbreviations 165
common prepositions 113
comparison of adjectives 56–63
comparison of adverbs 108
complement 92.3, 147

compound adverb 107.3
compound name 168
compound noun 23.6, 131.1(b), 162
compound preposition 112.1(b)
compound verb 106
compounding 162
conditional clause 159.3
conjugation 79–90
conjunction 133–6, 140
consonant 4–8
context 157
coordinating conjunction 133, 156.4(d)
copula verb 103.4
count noun 34

da 111.4, 134.2(b)
dash 174
date 65.2, 131.4
de 10, 67f
De 10, 67f
decades 65.6, 172.3
decimals 65.5
definite declension of the adjective 53
definite form of the adjective 44, 53f
definite form of the noun 22, 38
dem 67
demonstrative pronoun 53, 74
den 67f
denne (**dette**, **disse**) 74
deponent verb 104.3
der (adverb) 158
der (pronoun) 75f, 135.2, 135.8, 142, 156.4(c)
det 67f, 142, 153
difficult adverbs 111
difficult conjunctions 136
dig 10, 67, 70
diphthong 3
direct object 103.1, 147
direct speech 149.1, 174
do 82.2
dog 111.4
du 67f
during 127, 128.5
dårlig 59.1
dårligt (adv.) 108

efter 115
eftersom 134.2(b)
eller 133
emphatic topic 149.3
en (article) 22, 38
én (numeral) 64.6
end 61.2, 134.2(b)

et (article) 22, 38
ét (numeral) 64.6
exclamation mark 173
existential sentence 153
expletive 132.9
extra positions 141, 171.8

female suffixes 23.7
festival 168
finite verb 138, 143, 149
first conjugation 80
first element 162
flere 59.3
flest 59.3
for 127
for (conj.) 133, 136.2
for (prep.) 115, 116
for at 91.3, 134.2(b)
forbi 113
fordi 134.2(b)
formal subject 67.2, 142, 153
forrige 53n
forskellig 61.2
fourth conjugation 83
fra 117
fractions 65.5
frem 110.2
fremme 110.2
from 127
front article 53
full stop 172
future tense 98
FV1 clause 138.1
FV2 clause 138.1
før 135.3
første 53n, 62n
få (adj.) 58
få (pronoun) 78
få (verb) 89.1

gammel 59.1
ganske 122.2
gender 22f
gender rules 23
general subordinator 134.2(a)
genitive 37, 131, 175
gerne 108, 111.1
glottal stop ('stød') 11
go 89.1
god 45.2
godt (adv.) 108
gradation series 83–90
greetings 132
grov 48.3

grow 92.1
grå 48.2
guillemet 174
gå 89.1

han 67f
have 82.1
have (har, havde, haft) 82.1, 96f
hen 110.2
henne 110.2
her 156.4(a)
hinanden 71
hjem 110.2
hjemme 110.2
hos 113, 129.3
hun 67f
hv- question 77, 138.2, 139
hv- word 75, 77, 135
hvad 75, 77, 135
hvem 75, 77, 135.1
hver(t) 78
hverandre 71
hvilken 75, 77
hvis 75, 133(b), 135.7, 159.3
hvordan 135.1
hyphen 176

i 118
if 136.7
ikke 107.1, 111.2, 151, 160.3
imitation 132
imperative 101
impersonal passive 105.7
impersonal subject 69.3
in 127ff
ind 110.2
inde 110.2
indeclinable adjective 50
indefinite adjective 45–51
indefinite adjective constructions 51
indefinite article 22, 38
indefinite form of the noun 22, 28
indefinite pronoun 78
inden 134.2(b), 135.4
independent clause 157
indirect object 147
indirect question 134.2(a), 135.1
indirect speech 133(a)
infinitive 91, 144
infinitive marker 91.2
infinitive phrase 153
inflexion of superlative 62
ingen (intet, ingen) 78

ingenting 78
inseparable compound verb 106
interjection 132
interrogative pronoun 77
into 127
intransitive verb 96, 103, 153
inversion 138.2, 160.1
inverted commas 174
inverted word order 138.2
it 67f

ja 132.5
jaså 132.5
javel 132.5
javist 132.5
jo 111.4, 132.5
jo ... desto 134.2(b)
jo ... jo ... 134.2(b)
jovist 132.5

know 81
komme 90.3
kunne (kan, kunne) 10, 100

lang(t) 58
langt (adv.) 108, 111.3
lige 111.4
lige ... som ... 136.3
lige ... så 61.1
ligge 86.5
light elements 150, 156.4(a)
ligne 61.1
lille 48.1, 59.1
link position 140
live 79
loanwords 32
længe 108, 111.3

main clause 139–53
man 78
mange 59.1
masculine suffixes 23.7
may 100, 102.1
med 119
me(de)ns 134.2(b)
meget (megen) 55.1, 78
mellem 127
men 133.2, 135.6
mere 59f
mest 59f
mig 10, 70
mod 120
modal auxiliary verb 91.2, 100, 143

money 65.4
month 168
mood 100–3
MPT-adverbial 146
must 100
måtte (må, måtte) 100

nationality words 42, 55
natural topic 149.2
ned 110.2
nede 110.2
negative element 160
negative prefix 163.4
nej 132.6
nemlig 111.4
no 132.6
no (pronoun) 78
nogen (noget, nogle) 78
nok 111.4
non-count noun 33
non-finite verb 144
noun 22–43
noun declensions 24–28
noun plurals 24–32
noun with end article 22, 35f
nu 111.4
nu da 135.8
number 36
numerals 64f
når 134.2(b)

object 147, 160.4
object complement 147
object pronoun 150
of 37.7, 127, 131
ofte 108
og 12
om (adverb) 110.2
om (prep.) 121
omkring 111
omme 110.2
on 127ff
ond 59.1
op 110.2
oppe 110.2
ordinal number 64f
orthography 166–68
other adverbials 146
ought to 100
over 122
over

particle 106
partitive genitive 131.3

passive 104.1, 105, 152
passive agent 105, 146, 152
past participle 92, 143
past perfect tense 97
past tense 75, 95, 99, 143
patient 105.2
perfect tense 96, 99
personal pronoun 67f
plural forms of loanwords 32
plural forms of nouns 24–32
possessive pronoun 43, 72f
predicting plurals 25
prefix 163.2, 163.4
preposition 112–26
preposition, place 130
preposition, time 128–30
prepositional complement 112.2
present participle 93, 144
present tense 94, 99, 143
prohibition 91.2
pronoun 67–78
pronunciation 1–10
punctuation 170–76
punctuation marks 170
put 82.2
på 123

real subject 142, 153
reciprocal pronoun 71
reciprocal verb 104.4
reflexive possessive pronoun 73
reflexive pronoun 70, 150
reflexive verb 103.5
relative clause 75f, 154.2, 171.1
relative pronoun 75
restrictive relative clause 75f

-s form of the verb 104
-s genitive 37
-s passive 104.2, 105.4
s- link 162.2
say 82.2
second conjugation 81
see 85.3
selv 70
selvom 134.2(b)
separable compound verb 106
sgu 111.4
shall 98, 100
should 98, 100
siden (conj.) 134.2(b)
siden (prep.) 113
sidste 53, 63n

sig 10, 70
sikke(n) (sikket, sikke) 51
similarity 61
sin (sit, sine) 72f
skam 111.4
skulle (skal) 10, 98, 100
skønt 134.2(b)
som 77f, 135.8, 158
spelling 166–68
spelling reform 166
statement 138.2, 139
stiv 48.3
stop 4–5
stor 58
straight word order 138.2
stress 13–21
stressed affixes 18f
stressed syllables 17
strong verb 83–90
stød 11f
stå
subject 138, 140, 149, 156.2
subject complement 147
subject pronoun 67f
subjunctive 102
subordinate clause 154, 156–60, 170
subordinating conjunction 134,
   156.4(d)
suffix 163.2, 163.5
syllable loss 9.1
syllable stress 17
så 134.2(b)
så ... at 134.2(b)
så ... som 134.2(b)

tage 10, 84
take 84
-tal 65.6, 65.7
telephone number 65.1
telescope reduction 164.2
temperature 65.3
tense 94–99
that (conjunction) 136.8
that (demonstrative) 74
that (relative pronoun) 75
The English, etc. 55
think 79
third conjugation 82
this 74
through 127
til 124
til + genitive 46.2
time by the clock 66

tit 108
to 127
topicalisation 149
transitive verb 96, 103
trods 113
turde (tør, turde) 100
two-verb constructions 91.3

ud 110.2
ude 110.2
uden 135.6
under 127
under 125
undtagen 135.6
ung 58
unstressed **e** 1.5n, 9
unstressed object 156.4(a)
uses of tenses 99

var 10
ved 126, 129.3
vel (stressed) 108
vel (unstressed) 111.4
verb 79–106
verb forms 79–92
verb particle 106
verb tenses 94–99
ville (vil, ville) 100
vist 111.4
vowel 1–3
vowel changes in nouns 29
vowel length 2
vowel merger 9.2
være (er, var, været) 88.3, 96f
være passive 105.6
værre, værst 59.2

want to 100
weak verb 79–82
weekday 168
will 100
wish 101.2, 102, 138.2, 139
with 127
word class 137
word formation 161–65
word order 137–60
word stress 17

yes 132.5
yes/no question 138.2, 139

Å/å 166f